WONDERS OF MAN

CHATEAUX
OF THE LOIRE

By Christopher Hibbert

NEWSWEEK, New York

NEWSWEEK BOOK DIVISION

Edwin D. Bayrd, Jr.   *Editorial Director*
Mary Ann Joulwan   *Art Director*
Laurie P. Winfrey   *Picture Editor*
Eva Galan   *Assistant Editor*
Diane Raines Keim   *Picture Researcher*

Alvin Garfin   *Publisher*

WONDERS OF MAN
Milton Gendel   *Consulting Editor*

ENDSHEETS: *One of a series of tapestries depicting court life in the central Loire valley during the High Renaissance, "La Promenade" shows noble lords and ladies conversing in a bower of beautiful blooms.*

TITLE PAGE: *The familiar façade of Chambord, with its massive cylindrical towers and its profusion of chimneys, lanterns and dormers, catches the full light of the late afternoon sun—and reflects back a near-perfect double of its extravagant roofline on the still surface of an ornamental pond.*

OPPOSITE: *Agnès Sorel, the enchanting mistress of Charles VII, lies buried beneath the mighty walls of Loches castle, were a faded portrait provides inadequate testimony to the qualities that drew the ill-favored dauphin to his "Lady of Beauty."*

Library of Congress Cataloging in Publication Data

Hibbert, Christopher, 1924–
Chatteaux of the Loire.

(Wonders of man)
Bibliography: p.
Includes index.
1. Loire River Valley (France)—History.
2. Castles—France—Loire River Valley.   I. Title.
II. Series.
DC611.L81H5 1982   944'.5   81-86170
ISBN 0-88225-317-4

Printed and bound in Japan

Contents

Introduction

Along the curving hillsides and noble valleys
The châteaux are strewn like so many altars,
And in the majesty of the mornings and evenings,
The Loire and her vassals move through these allées.

To those who know the Loire valley only by reputation, Charles Péguy's reverential lines, penned shortly before his death in the first battle of the Marne, may seem high-flown. But to those who know the central Loire firsthand, they are both evocative and accurate. There is a certain natural majesty to the region, and the central valley is a kind of architectural temple, one that annually attracts hundred of thousands of pilgrims, all eager to inspect Péguy's "altars"—the dozens of splendid châteaux strewn along the banks of the Loire and her vassal tributaries. These range in size from the grandiose Chambord, whose 440 rooms once housed the retinue of that greatest of sixteenth-century princes, Francis I, to the modest but enchanting Plessis-Bourré, built for a nobleman who served as finance minister to one of Francis's predecessors. Taken together, these grand châteaux and smaller *châteaux de plaisance* tell, in stone, the glorious tale of the French Renaissance. They do not begin to tell the full history of the Loire valley, however, for it reaches back a full millennium before the first of these stately pleasure domes was erected. This is the Loire of the *châteaux fort*, the heavily fortified redoubts built by the first dukes of Anjou to withstand the depredations of Norse raiding parties and Saracen armies, English invasion forces and rebellious countrymen. To this category belong the supposedly impregnable Loches, which Richard the Lion-Hearted, bravest and most promising of Henry II and Eleanor of Aquitaine's four sons, took in a mere three hours; Chinon, whose ruined keep is forever associated with the most extraordinary warrior-maid in all history, Joan of Arc; and Langeais, whose tenth-century keep, erected by that untiring castle-builder Fulk the Black, is said to be the oldest in France.

Péguy may not have intended to include the famed fortress-towns of the central Loire valley among his altars, but these historic cities cannot fairly be excluded from the pilgrim's trail, for they too are a vital part of the region's history. There is Orléans, site of Joan of Arc's greatest victory. There is Tours, where Christianity took root under the watchful eye of a dedicated fourth-century bishop, St. Martin, and flourished under the cultivation of a talented historian, Gregory, and a brilliant teacher, Alcuin. And there is Angers, ancestral home of the counts of Anjou and their Angevin descendants, the Plantagenets and the Capets. All of these historic places and historical personages figure in the engrossing narrative that follows, but that story is by no means confined to castles and castle-builders. The Loire valley has long been a gastronomical temple as well—with famous vineyards and three-star restaurants its "altars"—and these products of "the garden of France" add savor to the ensuing tale.

THE EDITORS

THE LOIRE IN HISTORY

I

"The Garden of France"

By almost any standards, the valley of the Seine is more beautiful. Not more bountiful—that title can legitimately be claimed by the Loire valley, known since ancient times as "the garden of France"—but certainly more picturesque. The Seine has superior scenery, grand vistas and great variety, unsullied beauty of the sort that inspires painters and poets; only the most chauvinistic citizens of the Haute-Loire would claim otherwise. But the history of France—from its Celtic dawn through the high noon of the Bourbon kings—belongs to the Loire and the Loire alone.

Until Louis XIV, the self-styled Sun King, moved the center of his personal solar system to Versailles in 1682, the valley of the Loire—especially the section lying between Nevers in the east and Angers in the west—was the very heart of France: home of its nobility, center of its commerce, and nexus of its religious and intellectual life. Not surprisingly, the central Loire was also a battlefield and a boneyard, for its agricultural, architectural, and artistic riches were coveted by foreign despots and native princes alike. The serenity one encounters in the Loire valley today belies its sanguinary past: where lowing herds of Charollais cattle graze along the banks of the longest river in France, great armies once marched; and the visitor who knows his history can sense the presence of those ghostly hosts even now.

It was from the Celtic capitals of Tours and Orléans (see map, page 164-65) that Vercingetorix, chief of the Arverin Celts and leader of the Gauls, launched his campaign against Julius Caesar and his legions in 52 B.C. And it was from an encampment between Gien and Orléans, in the northernmost arc of the Loire, that the Carnutes maintained their dogged but foredoomed resistance to the conquering Romans. Tours, sixty miles to the west, was the scene of Charles Martel's stunning victory over the Saracens in A.D. 732, a date crucial not only to the history of the central Loire but to all of Western civilization. Martel's triumph over a superior Moorish force marked the end of Arab incursions into Western Europe and came at a time when Islam, which had already engulfed Iberia, seemed poised to sweep over the entire continent.

Little more than a century later the central Loire was to come under attack from a new enemy and a new direction. This time the foe were Norse pirates and their avenue of attack was the Loire itself. Moving up and down the river in their swift, shallow-draft *drakkars*, these Scandinavian freebooters preyed upon the hapless denizens of the Loire valley for decades. Armies were raised against them, notably by Robert le Fort at Angers, west of Tours, in 866; but it was many years before the raiders' depredations could be curbed. Driven at last from the central Loire, the Normans, as they were known in France, settled on the sparsely populated northwest coast, accepted Christianity, and converted their penchant for piracy into a talent for honest trading. From this base, they were to stage their successful invasion of England in the eleventh century.

In the feudal epoch that followed the expulsion of the Normans from the Loire valley, two great baronial houses were to arise—one at Blois, which lay below Orléans in the east; the other at Angers, in

the west. The territory that lay between them, the rich fief of Touraine, was avidly sought by both. Generations of internecine strife ensued, brought to an end only when Fulk the Black, count of Anjou and head of the Angevin line, succeeded in defeating Thibaut de Tricheur, count of Blois, and annexing all of Touraine. Had a descendant of Fulk the Black, one Goeffroy le Bel, not married the Norman Empress Maltida, heiress to both the province of Normandy and the whole of England, the central Loire might have enjoyed several decades of relative tranquility. Instead, this alliance, which gave rise to the Anglo-Angevin house of Plantagenet, was to embroil the heirs of Hugh Capet, count of Touraine, and those of the Plantagenet King Henry II in the self-defeating madness known as the Hundred Years' War.

The Angevin kings followed the course of this war, in large part, from their mighty fortress at Chinon, southwest of Tours. It was here that the Maid of Orléans, Joan of Arc, presented herself to the dauphin who was to become Charles VII and begged his permission to lead a relieving army against the English troops besieging Orléans. Under Joan's leadership the dauphin's armies would succeed in breaking the long stalemate that had produced only death and more death, not victory, and in time the English would be driven from French soil altogether. Peace came at last to the central Loire—and with peace, prosperity such as the region had never known. Inspired by the ideals of the Italian Renaissance and assisted by Italian artists and artisans, the Angevin nobility were to string a necklace of glittering new châteaux, ranging from the monumental Chambord to the exquisite Plessis-Bourré, across the entire central Loire.

Although many of these structures resembled the donjons of old in their superficial details, none were actual redoubts. They were peacetime dwellings, reflecting their builders' collective confidence—correct, as it happens—that the Loire valley would never again experience a major military campaign. It was at last possible, after sixteen centuries of contention, to turn the moldering bones of Celts and Romans, Franks and Saracens, French and English under, and to plant crops on the former battlefields with some assurance that it would be possible to harvest them. What was not possible was to forget the past, for by the time peace came at last to the central Loire a network of old and new fortifications dotted the valley: medieval keeps built on the remains of Roman encampments; feudal bastions like those at Blois, Tours, and Angers; fortress castles such as Chinon, Loches, and Sully; and solidly built Renaissance châteaux at Amboise, Chaumont, and Chenonceaux.

The result of a millennium and more of incessant building in response to unceasing strife, the architectural and historical wealth of the central Loire is staggering—and its true measure can only be suggested by the abbreviated tour that follows. If you do not choose to track the Loire all the way back to its source, high in the Vivarais Mountains of southeastern France, on the borders of the *départements* of Ardèche and Haute-Loire, you will never see all the châteaux of the Loire. You will, for example, be

Sully, the most easterly of Loire valley châteaux, is a fairytale castle with a fantastic history. Built in the twelfth century to guard a Loire bridgehead, the great keep served as home to Maurice de Sully, the bishop of Paris responsible for the rebuilding of Notre-Dame— and it served as a home away from home to Charles VII, who was in residence when Joan of Arc at last persuaded him to journey to Rheims to be crowned. Extensively renovated and enlarged by Maurice's successors—who dug the moats that now isolate the castle both from the Loire and from the surrounding countryside—Sully was witness to a steady procession of monied, titled, and gifted guests. Among the latter was François-Marie Arouet, exiled from Paris at the age of twenty-two for having incensed the regent with his acerbic wit. Young Arouet was to stage several of his early plays—one of them, Henriad, *written at Sully—in a small theatre set up on the first floor of the keep. The medallion at right was struck decades later, after Arouet had achieved international fame under his nom de plume, Voltaire.*

denied a chance to inspect the ruins of the château of Rochebaron, glowering down upon the small town of Bass-en-Basset at the conjunction of the Loire and one of its early tributaries, the Ance, thirty-odd miles southwest of Lyons. But the true Loire of the châteaux begins at Nevers, where a fifteenth-century ducal palace dominates the cityscape. Begun in the mid-1400s, it was finished in the sixteenth century by the Gonzagas of Mantua, into whose family it had passed on the marriage of Louis di Gonzaga to Henriette de Clèves, sister of the François de Clèves who was made duke of Nevers by King Francis I in 1539. Before setting forth from Nevers, take time to wander through the nearby Cathedral of St. Cyr and Ste. Juliette, built in a variety of styles from the eleventh to the sixteenth centuries and containing a captivating series of thirteenth-century figures crouching in painful poses to support the columns of the triforium.

From Nevers the Loire sweeps in a wide arc northwest to Orléans, taking in the waters of the Allier at le Bec d'Allier and passing beneath the Romanesque bell towers and abbey church of La Charité-sur-Loire and the vineyards around Pouilly-sur-Loire. Pouilly itself is on the eastern bank of the Loire, on the noisy, congested *route nationale* from Nevers to Paris. Better by far, then, to take the western bank, which has the additional advantage of taking you through Sancerre, a delightful town standing on higher ground than you will afterwards encounter on your way across the Loire valley.

From Sancerre follow the riverside road toward Cosne-sur-Loire, pausing at Buranlure to peer across the moat at the fourteenth-century walls and towers of its château before heading on to Gien, site of the oldest street fair in France. It was at Gien that Joan of Arc crossed the Loire on her way to assist in the coronation of Charles VII at Rheims, riding across the handsome bridge beneath the walls of Gien's beautiful brick château—now a museum of sporting guns and falconry. If you are interested in fishing, you should cross the river here to visit a museum devoted to its craft that has been installed in a seventeenth-century château at La Bussière in a park designed by the famed landscape architect André Lenôtre. If this does not appeal to you, keep to the western bank and make for Sully-sur-Loire.

At Sully the traveler will find the first of the grand châteaux of the Loire, the castle where Joan of Arc spent a month shortly before her capture at Compiegne; where Henry IV's minister, the duke of Sully, lived in extravagant splendor; and where, as a guest of a subsequent duke, Voltaire staged his early comedies. Sully has the added distinction of being one of the very few châteaux that actually stand on the banks of the Loire; the gentle waters have now receded, but as late as the seventeenth century they lapped the bases of the castle towers. A true feudal keep, Sully was extensively damaged by bombing in 1940 and 1944, but it has been largely restored.

Cross the river again at Sully and drive on to St. Benoît-sur-Loire, a delightful village that was once a town of more than 15,000 inhabitants living under the protection of the immense abbey, known in earlier times as the Abbaye de Fleury. Founded in the seventh century, the abbey was repeatedly damaged

by Norman raiders and was demolished after the Revolution; all that remains is the Romanesque church, which contains the bones of St. Benedict. The eleventh-century narthex of this church—the lower part of which forms a porch with narrow naves, groined vaults, and monumental pillars whose capitals bear carvings of unparalleled grace and elegance—is one of the most extraordinary structures of its period in all of France.

Continuing on the river road through Germigny-les-Prés, which boasts one of the oldest Romanesque churches in France, and through Chateauneuf-sur-Loire and Jargeau will soon bring you to Orléans and the heart of the country forever associated with Joan of Arc. But neither at Jargeau, where Joan won a savage battle against the English, nor at Orléans, where she achieved her greatest victory, are there any buildings left that can be associated with her. And unless you wish to see the rather humdrum Gothic Cathedral of the Holy Cross, which seventeenth- and eighteenth-century architects restored with a heavy hand, you will miss little by cutting off that loop of the Loire altogether and driving west through La Ferté-St. Aubin to the Loire-side town of Beaugency.

Beaugency is a pleasant small town with much of interest to see, and as you stand beneath the immensely tall, forbidding walls of its eleventh-century keep you will at last be able to feel the presence of Joan, for she, too, looked upon these thick gray walls as she rode along the riverbank, undetected by the keep's English garrison, to the beleaguered city of Orléans in May 1429.

If stones could speak, the saying goes, what stories they would tell. In the central Loire valley, many of those stories would be tragic ones. The brick and stone manor house at right, for instance, was where Leonardo da Vinci, the very embodiment of the Renaissance, spent the last years of his life—and where he died. And all that remains of the duke of Choiseul's splendid château at Chanteloup, built in imitation of Versailles, is its seven-tier, 144-foot-high stone pagoda, below, erected in 1775 at the height of the Continental craze for all things Chinese; the château itself, having fallen into disrepair, was demolished after the Revolution. Azay-le-Rideau, left, survived the Revolution virtually intact, but this elegantly proportioned and perfectly situated Gothic-style mansion is the second structure to stand on the site. The first was pulled down in 1418 on the orders

Above Orléans the Loire is almost sluggish, appearing rather like the estuary of a tidal river when the waters have fallen back into the sea. Numerous small islands, clumps of trees growing in the sandy bed, irregular mounds of rough, forlorn grass, and spatterings of rock break the still waters in which the bridges and riverside buildings are reflected as though in a millpond. The Loire narrows at Beaugency, however, and around the piers of the twenty-two arches that comprise its moss-encrusted bridge you will see the water frothing white.

You are now faced with a difficult choice: whether to continue your journey along the northern or southern bank of the river. For you are now entering the heart of the châteaux country, and most of the legendary châteaux—Chambord, Cheverny, Chaumont, Chenonceaux, Valençay, Loches, Villandry, Azay-le-Rideau, Ussé, and Chinon—are to the south. To give these grand monuments their due, it is best to stay for a few days in some convenient town and go out from there to see each of them as opportunity affords.

You might choose, for instance, to stay in Tours, where there are more comfortable hotels and more memorable restaurants than are to be found anywhere else in the valley. If you do make Tours your center, then you will have ample time to see its cathedral, built in a marvelous mixture of styles from the thirteenth to the sixteenth centuries and containing much lovely stained glass; the Basilica of St. Martin; and the well-preserved fifteenth-century wooden houses around the Place Plumereau. You will also be able to walk through the intriguing streets of the old town, miraculously preserved during the devastating bombardments of World War II, and to sit under the trees opposite the Île Simon, watching the Loire pass beneath the arches of the elegant eighteenth-century Pont de Pierre, renamed the Pont Wilson in honor of the American President whose army's administrative headquarters were here in World War I.

Leaving the countryside to the south of the Loire for a more prolonged visit, then, cross the bridge at Beaugency and take the road on the northern bank toward Blois, stopping en route at Ménars to see its handsome seventeenth-century château. This was built by a wealthy wine merchant and was subsequently enlarged and improved by King Louis XV's architect, Jacques-Ange Gabriel, for Mme. de Pompadour. (Among Gabriel's contributions to the interior are private apartments paneled in sculpted woodwork of unusually high caliber.) The formal gardens at Ménars are lined with boxtrees and filled with statues, vases, and follies, among them a Lovers' Temple with a perfectly rounded cupola. Ramps lead to the lower gardens and a columned grotto attributed to Soufflot, and these lower gardens run right down to the banks of the river itself.

Soon after leaving Ménars you will encounter the château of Blois, so much more impressive when seen from the courtyard than from the lower town; and half an hour later you will enter Amboise, whose château looms above you on the far side of the bridge. The spire of the little chapel of St. Hubert, patron of huntsmen, is appropriately decorated with antlers.

of Charles VII, who insisted he had been insulted by a member of the Burgundian guard housed at Azay. In his rage the Dauphin had the entire garrison hanged and the town torched, and for a century thereafter the site was known as Azay-le-Brulé—"Azay the Burned."

OVERLEAF: *Langeais, due north of Azay-le-Rideau, was built in 1465–67—a short period of time by contemporary standards; other châteaux took decades to complete. As a result, it has a unity of style that is rare in the Loire valley. Its unadorned façade is military in aspect, but that is not inappropriate, for the castle stands on the ruins of a Roman castrum. Moreover, its keep, said to be the oldest in the valley, was built by Fulk the Black in 994 for purely defensive purposes.*

In addition to the château at Amboise, you should see Le Clos-Lucé, the brick and stone fifteenth-century manor house at the top of the Rue Victor Hugo, where Leonardo da Vinci spent the last years of his life under the patronage of Francis I. Having been divided into smaller rooms with false ceilings and lath and plaster partitions in the nineteenth century, the manor house is now gradually being restored to its original appearance. The huge kitchen is as Leonardo must have known it; so is the bedroom where he died—traditionally in the arms of Francis I himself, as indicated by the picture on the bedroom wall and as movingly described in Vasari's *Lives of the Most Eminent Painters, Sculptors, and Architects.* (In actual fact the king was at St. Germain-en-Laye that day, celebrating the birth of the future Henry II.) In the basement of the manor house are several models of machines and inventions constructed from Leonardo's plans; and in the chapel, a fresco dubiously attributed to the master's hand.

Since you are now on the southern outskirts of Amboise, you might consider driving a few kilometers down the road toward Bléré and into the forest of Amboise. This forest boasts the extraordinary pagoda of Chanteloup, built by the duke of Choiseul, Louis XV's minister, who was exiled from court at the request of Mme. du Barry. This fanciful parody of *chinoiserie*, standing on a circular peristyle, is all that remains of the duke's enormous château. The top of the pagoda affords a splendid view of the Loire from Tours as far as Blois.

Returning to Amboise from Chanteloup, recross the bridge and turn right along the riverside road to

The great abbey of Fontevrault was founded in 1099 as both a nunnery and a monastery, with the sexes strictly segregated and the orders administered by a lone abbess. Over the centuries the abbey cloister was to shelter a number of repudiated queens and a host of renounced wives, rejected daughters, and pious widows—all of high birth and many destined to serve as abbess themselves. This aristocratic order flourished for 700 years before falling into disarray under the Empire, when Napoleon disbanded the order and converted Fontevrault into the prison it remained until 1963. One structure that has survived these vagaries of fortune virtually intact is the kitchen tower (opposite), a marvel of medieval design and engineering. From an octagonal base flanked by round apses the tower rises 88 feet to a basket funnel pierced for ventilation, the apex of a system of ducts and chimneys—twenty in all—that is as remarkable for its beauty as for its efficiency.

Tours. In a short time you will pass through Vouvray with its neat vineyards that have made the name of this undistinguished town so familiar. Just beyond Tours (headquarters for your more leisurely tour of the grand châteaux south of the Loire) you will come to Luynes. The village is dominated by a starkly impressive castle, much of which was built in the thirteenth century. Next is the village of Cinq-Mars-la-Pile, whose curious square tower of unknown origin and purpose—but usually attributed to the Gallo-Roman period—has puzzled scholars for centuries. And here there is another château that once belonged to Louis XIII's favorite, the marquis of Cinq-Mars. Unlike its neighbor at Luynes, it is open to the public and is well worth a visit for the lovely Gothic vaulting in the eleventh- and twelfth-century towers and for the views of the Loire downstream from Tours. Just beyond Cinq-Mars-la-Pile you will come to the pleasant small town of Langeais. In its center rises the massive château built by Louis XI's minister Jean Bourré, beside the remains of a huge donjon erected more than five centuries earlier by Fulk the Black. In truth the history of Langeais castle is as old as that of France itself. The name is thought to come from the Latin word for seagull, *alaegavia*, a bird still seen flying above this stretch of the Loire; and the appellation may commemorate a long-lost Roman settlement on the site. Bickered over by the counts of Blois and Anjou—and later by the Capetians and Plantagenets—this château became a den for English captains during the Hundred Years' War. Rebuilt by Bourré in the fifteenth century, Langeais was the site of Anne of Brittany's marriage to Charles VIII in December 1491. It is decorated with furnishings of that period, and its chimney pieces and tapestries are superb.

Beyond Langeais, cross the Loire at Port-Boulet and take the road that leads from Bourgueil to Chinon; then go on toward Saumur, turning off the road to see the abbey of Fontevrault. In the vast, plain, silent nave of this church the light streams down upon the polychrome tombs of those Plantagenet kings and queens of England who chose to be buried here. The guide will also show you the astonishing kitchen of the abbey, known as Evraud's Tower, a building as ingenious and practical as it is beautiful—with twenty chimney flues designed to take away smoke from the blazing fires. After you have seen the abbey, go look at its treasures, which include a high altar now transferred to the nearby Church of St. Michael.

Returning to the main road and making for Saumur, you will pass under the fifteenth-century white walls of the château of Montsoreau. This château is the setting of a novel by Alexandre Dumas *père*, *The Lady of Montsoreau*, which adds romantic embellishments to the story of the count of Montsoreau, who had his wife's lover murdered by hired assassins in her presence at La Coutancière on the opposite bank of the river.

Keeping to the left bank of the Loire and driving along at the foot of hills in which caves have been scooped out of the rock and turned into houses and cellars, you will soon reach Saumur. In the seventeenth century this was a large and prosperous center of Protestantism, when the town had some seven

If Angers castle is an archaeologist's dream, it is also an architect's nightmare. What stands today on the castle mount is a gallimaufry of disparate styles and building materials—an aesthetic hodgepodge that only begins to suggest the structure's fascinating history. The oldest stonework at Angers was laid down in the early 800's, when a redoubt was raised to repel invading Norman armies. Four centuries later these modest walls were buried beneath seventeen colossal white stone and slate towers, several nearly 200 feet high, which give the castle its distinctive silhouette. Within these daunting perimeter walls stand the château itself, its detached chapel, and this gatehouse, all that remains of a vanished royal residence.

thousand more inhabitants than it has now, two-thirds of the population having emigrated when the Huguenots' privileges were withdrawn by the revocation of the Edict of Nantes. Although the wine trade and the famous cavalry school have kept Saumur alive, it is still a quiet town whose Gothic château, which now contains an equine museum as well as a museum of decorative arts, seems strangely aloof from the violence of its history. Just below the château you will find the Church of Our Lady of Nantilly, a lovely Romanesque building adorned by a well-preserved thirteenth-century wooden statue of Our Lady and by many splendid tapestries.

All the fine tapestries you will have seen by now, however, appear almost insignificant when compared with the superb series to be seen in the castle at Angers. The main road to Angers is along the right bank of the Loire; and this is the road that many prefer since it passes the château of Boumois in the pretty little town of Les Rosiers. Although recently restored, this sixteenth-century structure is not particularly eye-catching—no match, at any rate, for its one-time mistress, who in 1646 inspired an admirer to carve these words into the paneling of the château's chapel: "Long live Madame du Boumois, the true mirror of perfection."

You will, at this juncture, almost certainly find the southern road, through Gennes and past the vineyards on the chalky slopes of the Saumur hills, the more rewarding. By going this way, you will be able to see the ruins of the great abbey of St. Florent, the town of Trèves with its famous tower (all that remains of a fifteenth-century castle), the remarkable

Romanesque church at Cunault, and the extraordinary fifteenth-century choir stalls in the church at Blaison. And you will enter Angers by the road that takes you directly into the square below the castle.

There is little left of Angers' castle, once the main stronghold of the counts of Anjou, other than the massive pile of walls and buttress towers that sprawl across the Place du Château like a stranded monster. But the chapel on top of these forbidding walls has been restored; so has the governor's house. And in a building specially constructed in 1952 are the astonishing series of tapestries depicting the Revelations of St. John the Divine, which were made by Hennequin of Bruges between 1373 and 1380, based on cartoons by Nicolas Bataille. You will want to spend as long as possible studying these superb works of art, but do not leave Angers without seeing the Gothic Cathedral of St. Maurice, which has some fine carvings and lovely stained-glass windows. Note also the charming fifteenth- and sixteenth-century houses around the Place Freppel, particularly the one known as Adam's House, which is carved with all manner of human figures, including the celebrated Angevin who lifts his shirt to reveal his genitals in a gesture at once scornful and lascivious.

If you leave Angers by the main road to Varades, you will be able to see two more splendid châteaux: Serrant, which was purchased in 1730 by James Walsh, grandson of the English seaman who transported the exiled King James II from England to France and afterwards made a fortune as a shipowner in Nantes; and Chamtocé, where Joan of Arc's companion Gilles de Rais, having retired from military life, gave himself over to those occult and revolting practices that led to his execution, in 1440, on an island in the middle of the Loire.

There are other, minor châteaux to the west of Angers, notably the feudal castle of La Flèche, where the Bourbon King Henry IV, who had been conceived at the castle, was to found a Jesuit college of considerable renown that numbered René Descartes and Éugene of Savoy among its graduates. But here our tour must end. West of La Flèche the consequential structures are further and further between, and the rewards of touring are no longer greater than the effort. It is time to abandon this itinerary for another, one that leads us back to a time when the banks of the Loire were inhabited not by châteaux builders but by a simpler sort of people who had neither need for great castles nor the skills to build them.

Once topped with two-story machicolations surmounted by pepper-pot roofs, the towers of Angers (below) were dismantled to the level of the castle's curtain-wall during the Wars of Religion in the sixteenth century. Happily, the fortress's legendary tapestries, woven in Paris two centuries earlier and donated to Angers by Louis I of Anjou, survived this troubled time and are housed today in a museum within the castle compound. Known collectively as the **Apocalypse Tapestry**, these seventy panels measure more than sixteen feet in height and 550 feet in length, making them not only the oldest but also the largest of medieval arras. At near left is the panel entitled "The Adoration of the Beast," while at far left is a detail of the panel's central figure, a many-headed leonine monster.

29

II

Land of Saint Martin

In the upper valley of the Loire, fifty-six years before the birth of Christ, an intimidating army of Roman legionnaries marched purposefully along the river's banks. The men wore cuirasses of leather and metal over sleeveless woolen shirts. Strips of cloth were bound around their calves, and glittering helmets covered their heads. They carried oval shields and barbed javelins six feet long. Most were armed with swords and daggers and many carried the hand mills with which they ground grain to make the rough bread that was their staple diet. Tough and well-disciplined, these were the elite troops of Julius Caesar's army—sent to subdue those dissident Celts whose leaders were displaying a growing animosity toward their Roman masters. They expected to have little trouble in dealing with such pockets of resistance as they would encounter in the upper valley.

There were, in all, some two hundred tribes of Celtic Gauls in the Loire valley and surrounding regions. Their ancestors had migrated across the Rhine eight hundred years earlier, settling in the rich lands between the Seine and the Garonne and displacing the earlier inhabitants, whose megaliths can still be seen in several places in the valley of the Loire. The Celtic Gauls were competent farmers and traders, a civilized people expert in painting pottery, making mirrors, and composing ballads. They minted their own coins and made swords of a quality only the Spaniards could match. Although brave and hardy, they were too impetuous and undisciplined to make good soldiers; and until 56 B.C. it had not been difficult to keep them subjected by

maintaining garrisons at Angers, Tours, and Orléans in the central Loire valley. In that year, however, there had been serious trouble with the Veneti, a bellicose tribe living to the north of the Loire estuary along the Atlantic coast. The Veneti had encouraged neighboring tribes to join with them in refusing to obey the orders of Roman officials and requisitioning officers, and two Roman administrators had actually been kidnapped and held for ransom. A full-scale revolt in Gaul seemed imminent.

Determined to deal with the troublemakers before they got out of hand, Caesar had ordered an army to march through the valley to crush them. His order proved easier to issue at Angers, where he made his headquarters, than to carry out in the field, however, for as his cohorts marched westward along the riverbank they observed that the estuary was filled with huge oak barges whose flat bottoms enabled them to negotiate the river's treacherous shallows with ease and whose leather sails were capable of surviving the worst Channel storms. These rude but serviceable vessels gave the Celts the advantage of extreme mobility, both in attack and retreat. Caesar's army could not subdue an enemy it could not catch, of course. And after Caesar himself had studied the Celtic barges from the banks of the Loire, he returned to Angers convinced that no headway could be made against the Veneti until he had built a fleet of similar vessels. His shipwrights were immediately set to work, and before long the conqueror of Gaul had at his disposal a considerable armada of flat-bottomed boats equipped not only with leather sails but with oars and—most ingenious of all—

sharp hooks mounted on the ends of long poles.

This imperial armada set sail downriver to engage the Celtic fleet, which had been sighted in the Gulf of Morbihan. Waiting until the wind had dropped and the Venetis' boats were drifting helplessly in the becalmed waters, the Roman commander gave orders that his own boats should be rowed toward the Celtic barges. As the Roman vessels drew alongside, Caesar's sailors grabbed up the long poles lying on deck, slashed through the enemy's lanyards with the hooks, jumped aboard the Celtic barges, and captured those Veneti they did not slay. The last of the insurgents were thus forced to surrender, and Caesar wasted no time in executing their leaders.

For a time there was an uneasy peace in the central Loire valley. But two years after the defeat of the Veneti fleet at Morbihan there was more trouble in Gaul, this time farther upriver at Orléans, where the Carnutes were to assassinate the king Caesar had appointed to rule over them. The violence soon spread: a Roman garrison in the central valley was massacred; and a Roman commander was struck to the ground by a Celtic leader, Ambiorix, who first tore the clothing from the hapless commander's back with the words, "How can creatures like you hope to rule over great men like us?" Declaring that he would not shave or have his hair cut until vengeance was his, Caesar marched into Gaul once more. Ambiorix escaped capture, but Acco, the chief of the Senones, was arrested in his place, stripped of his clothes, lashed to a crude pillory, beaten to death with rods, and decapitated.

Enraged rather than intimidated by Caesar's retri- bution—which many of them had been obliged to witness—other Celtic chieftains swore to retaliate as soon as they could. First the Carnutes turned on the Roman community in Orléans, murdering all its members. Then the Averni rose in revolt under their brilliant commander, Vercingetorix, a former officer in Caesar's cavalry whose leadership was accepted by several other tribes. Well aware of the danger and extent of this new uprising, Caesar returned immediately to Gaul and laid siege to Bourges, the capital of the Bituriges tribe, whose lands lay between the Loire and its tributary the Cher, southeast of Orléans. The surrounding countryside had been laid waste on the orders of Vercingetorix, who realized that the only hope of defeating the Romans lay in denying them supplies. But the Bituriges, having burned to the ground twenty of their outlying settlements, begged Vercingetorix to allow them to spare Bourges itself; they insisted that their capital could easily be defended against Caesar's armies since the only approach to it was a narrow causeway over marshy ground. Believing their confidence to be misplaced, Vercingetorix unwillingly agreed to the Bituriges' request—and his doubts about the impregnability of their capital proved justified. After siege operations lasting less than a month, Bourges fell to the legionnaries and its inhabitants were indiscriminately slaughtered.

Caesar now moved his supply base to Nevers, at the eastern end of the central Loire region, and there prepared to lead an attack on Vercingetorix's main fortress, a powerful stronghold on a plateau near the Loire's juncture with the Allier. The Ro-

man assault failed to dislodge the Averni chieftain and his followers; instead, seven hundred Roman foot soldiers and almost fifty centurions were killed in one of the most humiliating reverses of Julius Caesar's entire military career. And, to make matters worse, the victorious Gauls now fell upon the Roman base at Nevers, wiped out the garrison, seized its supplies, and burned the town.

These Celtic successes in the central Loire were not matched elsewhere in Gaul, and when a strengthened Roman army forced Vercingetorix to capitulate near the source of the Seine the Gallic revolt collapsed. By 51 B.C. the uprising was over, the last band of Celtic insurrectionists being overwhelmed at Puy d'Issolu, where those who survived the battle had their hands cut off as a lesson to their countrymen. Gaul became a province of the Roman empire—and so it remained for five centuries.

Although the peasants in the countryside and the poorer workers in the towns along the Loire were initially slow to adapt to the ways of Rome, the whole of Gaul eventually accepted the civilization of the conquerors and became part of it. Towns were built on the Roman model; citizens dressed themselves in Roman fashions; traders and merchants learned to discuss their business in Roman terms. All along the banks of the Loire the remains of this Roman civilization can still be seen. Parts of a Roman wall are preserved behind the ducal palace at Nevers, for instance, and what remains of a Roman arcade can be found near the prefecture at Angers. The remnants of a huge amphitheater stand at Gennes; and there is even a Roman tower beside the cathedral at Tours.

Tours, indeed, was one of the most important Roman towns, not only in the central Loire valley but in the whole of Gaul. The original Celtic town, capital of the Turones tribe, had been built on high ground on the right bank of the river (near what is today the suburb of St. Symphorien). On the opposite bank the Romans built their settlement, called Caesarodunum until the beginning of the fifth century, when it was changed to Civitas Turonum. As early as the third century it became a Christian center through the preaching of St. Gatien, to whom its first cathedral was dedicated. After Gatien's death, however, paganism once more took hold at Tours, and Christian priests were obliged to take refuge in the grottoes on the right bank of the river. A century was to pass before another remarkable man came to Tours to combat the heathenism.

This man was St. Martin. Born in what is now Hungary and educated in Italy, Martin had joined the Roman army as a young man and was sent to serve in Gaul. One day, as an eighteen-year-old soldier on duty in Amiens, he had come across a beggar shivering in his rags. So moved was Martin by the man's plight that he cut his cloak in two with his sword and wrapped half of it around the man's shoulders. A few years later, following his conversion, Martin asked to be released from the army, declaring that he was now "Christ's soldier."

After a period spent as a recluse on the desert island of Gallinaria near Genoa, Martin joined the followers of the learned but contentious St. Hillary, bishop of Poitiers, as an exorcist. It was while he was with St. Hillary that he founded the monastery at Ligugé, near Poitiers—the first monastery in all of Gaul. By now Martin's fame as a preacher, his zeal, and his purity of heart had become known to the Christians of Tours, who invited him to become their bishop and help them in their fight against the heathen gods that were once again being worshiped in their city. Martin did not hesitate, and soon pagan temples were being pulled to the ground in Tours, idols were being smashed, and people were turning by the hundreds to the Christian faith so eloquently and passionately preached by the young bishop.

Not content with sermons and conversions, Martin built numerous churches along the Loire; and by the gates of Tours itself he founded the abbey of Marmoutier. What little remains of the abbey can be seen on the north bank of the Loire just east of St. Symphorien, site of Celtic tours. St. Gatien himself is said to have celebrated his first mass in the cruciform excavation known as the Chapel of the Seven Sleepers, resting place of seven of Martin's disciples, all of whom died on the same day—precisely as their spiritual leader had predicted. Some years later Martin retired to the village of Candes at the confluence of the Loire and the Vienne, between Saumur and Chinon. There he passed the remaining years of his life in prayer and contemplation, dying in the small cell that was his study in November 397.

No sooner had word of Martin's death reached Ligugé than the monks of the monastery he had founded there came to Candes to claim his body, but the monks of Marmoutier reached the village first. They seized Martin's corpse in the dead of night, carried it down to a boat moored at the river's

edge, and rowed back to Tours in the early morning light. As they bore their beloved burden to its final resting place, the monks reported, the wintry landscape miraculously changed its appearance: the dead and dying foliage turned green again, flowers appeared in the grass, and birds began to sing. This first "St. Martin's summer" was far from being the only miracle for which the saintly relics of St. Martin were given credit. The sick and maimed were assured that if they made a pilgrimage to the Basilica of St. Martin at Tours and touched the tomb containing the saint's holy bones they would arise cured and whole. One of Martin's early disciples even composed a short biography to which was appended a list of the miracles wrought beside the saint's tomb, and copies of this work were distributed all over Europe, North Africa, and the Near East. Pilgrims came from far and wide, and the town of Tours grew larger and more prosperous as, year after year, their number increased.

But even as Tours prospered the Roman empire gradually collapsed and Gaul was overrun by numerous bands of barbarian invaders from the east. Of these invaders, the Visigoths and the Franks proved to be the most powerful. At the beginning of the sixth century the leader of the Franks was Clovis, an unprincipled warrior who became a Christian under the influence of his devout wife, Clotilda, a Burgundian princess. In 507 Clovis marched against the Visigoths, killed their king, Alaric, with his own hand in a decisive battle near Poitiers, and drove them south across the Pyrenees. Having added their territories to his own, Clovis received the insignia of a Roman consul from the Eastern Roman emperor, now established at Constantinople, who chose to consider himself heir to the authority of the extinct Western Empire.

After Clovis' death in 511, his sons continued to expand the Frankish kingdom, and by the middle of the sixth century it extended as far as the Pyrenees, the Alps, and the Rhine. At the heart of this huge kingdom, on the road between the north and south of Frankland, Tours continued to thrive as a convenient stopping place for travelers and as a center of religion and learning. Its reputation was much enhanced in this period by Georgius Florentius, later known as St. Gregory of Tours. Gregory had arrived in Tours as a newly ordained deacon, seeking a cure at the tomb of St. Martin for a serious illness from which he was suffering. An attractive young man from a wealthy family, Gregory soon became universally liked and respected in Tours, where he lived with his uncle, the bishop Euphronius. And, on Euphronius' death in 573, thirty-five-year-old Gregory was appointed his successor.

Now best known as the first of French historians, author of the famous *History of the Franks*, Gregory was renowned in his own lifetime as a talented administrator, a brilliant propagandist of the cult of St. Martin, and a munificent patron. Under his guidance and protection a large abbey was built around the Basilica of St. Martin, an abbey that was to become immensely rich, principally through land holdings in France and several foreign countries.

Yet, ordered and untroubled as life generally was in Tours, such was not the case in other parts of

Frankland. The Merovingian dynasty—so named after Clovis' legendary grandfather, Merovech—ruled the kingdom for three hundred years, but the triumphs of Clovis himself were never to be repeated. Constantly at war with each other, his heirs tore their inheritance apart. Laws were forgotten or disregarded; brigandage was rampant; Latin culture was despised; schools were closed. Effete, debauched, brutal, corrupt, the Merovingian kings sank lower into a slough of vice. Even Dagobert, the least degenerate of the Merovingians, died "of old age" when he was thirty-four. After his death the dynasty was doomed; power passed into the hands of the so-called mayors of the palace, hereditary officials whose influence passed from father to son, generation after generation.

This family of officials was known collectively as the Pepin. Pepin the Old had been succeeded in the 640s by Pepin of Herstal; Pepin of Herstal by Charles Martel, a fine soldier who was virtual ruler of Frankland for twenty-six years. During this period Martel trained a formidable army—with which he was able to resist the increasingly bold encroachments of the Arabs, who had conquered Iberia and were intent upon extending their empire north of the Pyrenees. In 732 a Saracen army invaded Frankland, advanced as far as Poitiers, and threatened to cross the Loire at Tours. Leading his army out to defend Tours, Martel not only checked the Saracens' advance but sent their horsemen scuttling back to Spain. It was a triumphant blow for Christendom, and the pope responded by rewarding Martel with the keys to the tomb of St. Peter in Rome.

At the same time he offered to recognize Martel as official Protector of the Roman Church—supplanting the Eastern emperor, who, from his palace in Constantinople, could do little to save the papacy from the menace of the Lombards. Martel chose to decline this honor, but his son, Pepin the Short, did undertake to deal with the Lombards—on the condition that the pope recognize him as king in place of the last of the Merovingians, Childeric III.

Having received papal permission for this dynastic change, Pepin the Short issued orders for Childeric to be packed off to a monastery and for his hair to be cropped—long hair being an age-old symbol of royalty among the Franks, the flowing locks calling to mind the rays emanating from the Sun God. King Pepin, a warrior like his father, fulfilled his promise to the pope by driving the Lombards from central Italy. He also conquered southwestern France, then known as Aquitaine, and he would almost certainly have extended his dominions still further had he not contracted a fatal fever in 768. He was taken to the tomb of St. Martin in Tours; but his prayers were unavailing. It was left to his son to continue the work that Pepin the Short had begun.

This son was Charlemagne. A tall young man with fair hair and arresting eyes, he was vital, ambitious, hard-working, and masterful. Much was expected of him, and even more was achieved. At first he had to share his inheritance with a brother; but after his brother's death, Charlemagne became master of almost all that is now France, Belgium, and the Netherlands, as well as parts of Germany and Switzerland. Thus the whole of the Loire, from the

Atlantic to the mountains, came under his rule.
Charlemagne had a vision, though, of an even greater empire, a Christian empire to replace that of the
Caesars, an empire that would stretch south of
the Alps into Lombardy and beyond the Rhine to
the Vistula. And this great empire, he hoped, would
one day be a place of beauty, culture, and learning.

Charlemagne conceived this ambition on a visit to
Rome in 774, and on his return to Frankland he
made his court into a center for scholars and artists
from all over Europe. He particularly welcomed
men from Italy and England; and he was anxious,
above all, to persuade the English scholar Alcuin to
leave York, where he was director of studies at the
influential cathedral school. Charlemagne pressed
Alcuin to cross the English Channel and help him
revive learning on the Continent, to teach the
Franks Latin, to open new schools and assemble
libraries. Alcuin eventually accepted the invitation
and settled at Charlemagne's court, where he became not only his master's close friend but also his
principal adviser in cultural matters and educational
policies throughout his domains.

Toward the end of Alcuin's life Charlemagne re-
warded him by making him abbot of the rich monastery at Tours where, relieved from the burden of
political matters, he could devote himself to learning and, in particular, to the improvement and enlargement of the writing rooms of the monasteries
under his jurisdiction. In these *scriptoria* at Tours
and other monasteries along the Loire—notably at
St. Benoît, whose monastic schools were founded by
Theodulf, bishop of Orléans—manuscripts of un-

surpassed beauty were produced, compiled in that
graceful Carolingian script which Charlemagne himself endeavored to perfect, and delicately illuminat-
ed. Students and craftsmen flocked to Tours, whose
reputation as a center of art and learning, as well as
of pilgrimage, had never stood higher.

In 800 Charlemagne visited Tours in the course
of a lengthy progress around his empire, and there
he held many discussions with Alcuin about the
development of the abbey schools and education in
general. While at Tours, he was offered homage by
the nobles of Brittany, descendants of those Chris-
tianized Celts who had settled in the area formerly
known as Armorica after being driven out of Britain
in the fifth and sixth centuries by the Anglo-Saxons.
But the satisfaction Charlemagne felt at having extended still further his already vast authority was
overcast by his grief at the death of the last of his
five wives, the lovely Liutgard. In great sorrow
Charlemagne continued his journey alone; and in
Rome on Christmas Day, when the grateful pope
placed a golden crown on his head, the king of the
Franks was saddened by the thought that Liutgard
could not share this triumphant moment with him.
The congregation rose to shout, "Long life and
victory to Charles Augustus, crowned by God, the
great and pacific emperor of the Romans!" The
Western Roman Empire had at last been revived.

But Charlemagne was fifty-eight years old in 800,
and his life—already long by contemporary standards—was nearing its end. Many doubted that his
vast empire could long survive him. Unwieldy and
vulnerable to attack, it could not have lasted long

even if his descendants had not divided it up among themselves according to Frankish custom. In 843, twenty-nine years after Charlemagne's death, they did precisely that, however. All of Frankland west of the Rhône and Saône rivers—a territory including the whole of the Loire valley—went to Charlemagne's grandson Charles the Bald.

The Carolingian inheritance of Charles the Bald was not an enviable one. The Saracens continued to attack from the south, making forays along the coast; and there was a new threat from the north. Out of the dark forests of Denmark and Norway, rapacious predators had crafted swift "dragon boats" and set sail in them in search of warmer lands. These Norsemen, or Normans as they came to be known in France, had penetrated the Seine as far as Paris and had made raids up other French rivers, including the Loire. Having established themselves in what is now Normandy, these pirates increasingly turned their attention toward the rich valley of the Loire. They sailed up from Nantes as far as St. Benoît-sur-Loire, pillaging the Benedictine abbey and forcing the monks to flee to Orléans. In 867 they seized Angers and remained there for twenty years until Charles the Bald, aided by the duke of Brittany, dug a canal to divert the waters of the river and forced them to retire for fear their boats would be left high and dry. At Tours the basilica, the abbeys, and twenty-eight churches were all burned down; and St. Martin's bones had to be taken to a place where the Normans could not find them. In the countryside wild animals roamed undisturbed; brigands were as numerous as they had been in the days of the barbarian invasions; peasants sought work inside the protection of town walls while tangled undergrowth spread across the fields.

With no central government capable of protecting them, people turned to the local lords whose forbidding castles—built as strongholds against the Norman invaders and serving as storehouses, barracks, prisons, and administrative offices—now covered the land on both banks of the river. Looming over the waters, these castles boasted tall stone keeps encrusted with wooden galleries on which guards stood watch, ready to defend them from attack. The power of these local lords in the lands they controlled was absolute. Many of them were more powerful, in fact, than the Carolingian kings, whose influence was steadily diminishing. When the last of the Carolingian line, Louis V, died childless in 987, the lords of the central Loire decided that the crown should be offered to Hugh Capet, a descendant of Robert the Strong, one of the greatest landowners in central France. Thus the so-called Capetian dynasty came into existence. The first Capets, though kings of France, had very little influence beyond the area around Paris known as the Île de France, the only territory they personally and directly controlled. The lords of the counties and duchies beyond their borders were their vassals in feudal theory, and were required to render them homage. But they obeyed royal commands issuing from the Île de France only when it suited them to do so, and the first Capetian monarchs were powerless to rebuke them. Among the most willful and independent of these vassals were the counts of Anjou.

III

Satan's Brood

The counts of Anjou came from the devil, it was said, and to the devil they would return. As St. Gerald relates in his chronicles, there was once a count of Anjou who came home to the central Loire valley from his travels in distant lands, bringing with him a bride as strange as she was beautiful. No one knew where he had found her, or who her parents were, or what thoughts passed through the mind behind that lovely yet disturbing face. She rarely went to church, it was noted, but when she did she invariably murmured some excuse to her attendants and left before the central mysteries of the Mass were celebrated. One day, as she turned to leave at the beginning of the Consecration, four of her husband's knights trod on the hem of her gown to prevent her from leaving. Twisting her face away from the altar, she struggled to escape; and as the priest raised the Host before the congregation, she let forth a fearsome scream. Then, still screeching, she tore herself free of her pinioned robe, clutched her two children in her naked arms, and flew out of the church through an open window—never to be seen again. The people of the area whispered that she was Melusine, daughter of Satan, a vampire who could not bear to look upon the body of Christ. She had taken two children with her, but two had been left behind—and from these two were descended the counts of Anjou, lords of the central Loire, masters of Angers: Satan's brood.

The counts of Anjou emerged into history from legend in the ninth century. At that time a local ruler whose name was Ingeler extended his family's holdings by marrying Aelendis of Amboise; and

their son, Fulk the Red, further increased this domain by marrying Roscilla, daughter of the lord of Loches. In striking contrast to both his forebears and his descendants, the next count, Fulk II, was a mild-mannered, deeply religious man who put away his armor to become an honorary canon of St. Martin's Basilica at Tours. He was known as Fulk the Good, and countless tales were told of his benignity.

One day, so contemporary chronicles have it, Fulk the Good came across a crippled leper in the streets of Tours. Unhesitatingly, Fulk picked the diseased creature up and carried him to the shelter of St. Martin's. At the door of the church the leper suddenly vanished. Later that night St. Martin himself appeared in a vision before Count Fulk as the latter celebrated Mass to tell him that, like St. Christopher, he had been granted the blessing of carrying on his own back the holy body of the Lord Jesus. This man of sanctity was apparently a man of lively spirit as well, for another contemporary tale has Louis IV coming down from Paris to visit Fulk the Good at Angers and discovering his host dressed not in the robes of a count but in the simple surplice of a chorister. The king's teasing remarks about Fulk's unusual choice of costume were silenced by the rejoinder, "You know, my lord, an ignorant king is only a crowned ass."

Fulk the Good's son Geoffrey, known as Greygown, has left no such stories to be remembered by, but his grandson, Count Fulk III, called "the Black," rampages through the history of the Loire valley like a raging fire. By his marriage to Elizabeth, heiress to Vendôme, he followed the family tradition of ex-

tending its possessions by choosing brides rich in land and money. Yet Fulk the Black preferred to gain his ends by the sword rather than by contract. Ambitious, vicious, violent, and grasping, he seemed content only when at war. He is encountered again and again in the chronicles of the time: terrifying enemies, rivals, and rebels all along the Loire, and building castle after castle to keep what he had won.

At Langeais he built a huge fortress, the dark, forbidding walls of whose ruined keep can still be seen on the grounds of the fifteenth-century château that supplanted both Fulk the Black's donjon and a fourth-century church founded by St. Martin himself. The château was built all of a piece during a five-year period, which is itself unusual among Loire valley châteaux. Even more unusual is the fact that it has not been added to or extensively remodeled since. Langeais is worth a visit, then, for its architectural purity—and also for the chance it provides to inspect what remains of Fulk's keep.

Fulk the Black is also responsible for the great castle at Trèves, with its 100-foot-high tower, and for extending and fortifying the castle of Chaumont. Nothing remains of the latter, however, for Fulk's bastions were demolished in the fifteenth century to make way for the grand château of the Amboise family, completed in 1510 by Charles II, who served Louis XII as Grand Master of the King's Household and, later, as Admiral of France. Fulk the Black acquired Chaumont from a vassal of the count of Blois; from this same vassal he took the castle of Saumur, which sits on a sheer promontory southeast

of Angers, and had its already substantial fortifications extended. Altogether, some twenty keeps in Anjou and Touraine are believed to have been built or enlarged at Fulk's command.

It is not castles alone that mark Fulk the Black's reign over Anjou, however. Often, his conscience pricked by some act of deceit or cruelty, he would build a church or monastery by way of atonement. He founded the Church of St. Aubin at Blaison and the abbeys of Notre-Dame-de-la-Charité and St. Nicolas at Angers, and he rebuilt the Carolingian Church of St. Martin and several other churches along the Loire from Saumur to Amboise. When his troubled conscience could not be cleared through church-building, Fulk would have himself dragged behind a horse and then flogged until the blood ran down his naked back. He made numerous pilgrimages as acts of expiation, and he even took part in a crusade to the Holy Land, where he is said to have torn off part of Christ's tomb with his teeth. In 1004 he founded the abbey at Beaulieu-lès-Loches to house this holy fragment, and it is there that he planned to be buried. Death would not find Fulk the Black for another thirty-six years, however, and during the intervening period he rarely left the central Loire at peace for long. At the age of seventy, for example, he celebrated his fiftieth year as count of Anjou by riding out of his castle at Angers to fight a battle at Saumur, galloped hard all the way, joined the fray, fought until his forces carried the day, and then rode back to his castle without a rest. Small wonder that the whole of the Loire breathed a sigh of relief when he died in 1040.

The Loire valley has spawned few characters more repellent—or more fascinating—than Fulk the Black, the eleventh-century count of Anjou described as "ambitious and unscrupulous, criminally violent, greedy and grasping." A sociopath of seemingly inexhaustible energy, Fulk the Black conducted a relentless campaign of conquest and castle-building in the Loire valley for half a century. His legendary appetite for battle—which lasted well into his sixth decade—led to the annexation of Touraine; his equally gargantuan appetite for building led to the construction of at least twenty keeps and numerous churches. Most of these, like the ruined donjon at left, are little more than empty shells today. The roof of the abbey of Aiguevive collapsed long ago, but the exquisite west portal (right) stands as tribute to the skill of Angevin masons.

Fulk the Black's descendants further enlarged the Angevin inheritance—which, with Fulk V's marriage to Aremburg of Maine in the first decade of the twelfth century, extended as far north as the border of Normandy. Trouble between Fulk and his new neighbor, Henry I, king of England and duke of Normandy, was averted in 1119 by a marriage between Henry's son William and Fulk's daughter Matilda. And when William was lost in a shipwreck soon thereafter, tensions were again averted by a state marriage, this time joining Henry's daughter Maud, the twenty-six-year-old widow of the German emperor, and Fulk's fifteen-year-old son Geoffrey.

Handing over his European possessions to Geoffrey, Count Fulk now rode off to Palestine, where the long-time widower married the daughter of the king of Jerusalem and, on his father-in-law's death in 1131, was crowned king of Jerusalem himself. He thus added further glory to his family's name and provided his descendants with what little excuse they needed to meddle in the affairs of the Holy Land. Left behind in Anjou, Geoffrey proved himself more than capable of taking care of his rich inheritance. Unlike the rest of his ill-favored family, he was extremely good-looking; he was also tough, calculating, and boundlessly energetic—as befitted the progenitor of the Plantagenets, as his heirs were to be known. The appellation was bestowed upon Geoffrey and his issue because of his habit of wearing in his hat a sprig of *genet*, or broom plant, "which in early summer makes the open country of Anjou and Maine a blaze of living gold," in the words of one contemporary historian.

Immediately following the death of his father-in-law, Henry I, Geoffrey invaded Normandy, and in 1144 he had himself crowned duke of Normandy in Rouen cathedral. Five years later he handed over the duchy to his promising son, Henry, who was then but sixteen. The trust his father reposed in Henry was not misplaced; indeed, Henry was to prove one of the most remarkable men of his time. Short and rather fat, with a big round head covered with reddish hair cropped so short that it was little more than bristle, he was far from prepossessing. His gray eyes were prominent and often bloodshot; his hands were large and coarse; his skin, red and freckled; his short legs, bowed and frequently blistered from long hours spent in the saddle. Moreover, his demeanor was almost demoniac. He could not bear to be still, and he conducted all his business standing up, pacing restlessly and talking in a harsh, cracked voice. He sat only to eat, and he ate little and impatiently. Even during Mass, it was reported, he fidgeted and scratched himself as he scribbled notes and messages.

For all this Henry was as learned as he was athletic—a brilliant administrator and a gifted linguist said to possess a knowledge of "all the languages from the French sea to the Jordan." He would stay up half the night arguing, then rise at dawn to ride out on business or hunt with ferocious zest. He claimed that he rode fast to keep his weight down, but at least one of the chroniclers at his court thought it was to dispel his erotic thoughts. Henry's sexual appetite was certainly voracious, and his mistresses were legion both before and after his mar-

riage to Eleanor of Aquitaine, the divorced wife of Louis VII of France.

Eleanor was as remarkable as her husband. The daughter of Duke William X of Aquitaine, she was eight years older than Louis, a passionate, romantic, witty woman of commanding personality. She had been married to the king of France as a caustic girl of fifteen, and she had made his life a misery. He was not worth a rotten apple, she used to say, deriding his reserved manner, his simple tastes, his religiosity that made him "more like a monk than a king." The retired, devotional life held no appeal for Eleanor: she had no patience with mild advocates of the cloisters, turning with relief to the militant exhortations of the fiery Cistercian St. Bernard. And when her husband, overcome with remorse on learning that certain mercenaries in his pay had burned down a cathedral, decided to do penance by taking the Cross, Queen Eleanor promptly informed him that she would accompany him on the crusade.

She ordered armor for herself and her ladies and took off for Jerusalem, giving observers the impression that she was the leader of the crusade rather than her husband, who had had his long hair cut off so that he now not only behaved like a monk but also looked like one. In contrast to King Louis, Queen Eleanor was determined to enjoy herself in the Holy Land; and enjoy herself she certainly did. She galloped about with her ladies, disrupting the army's movements; she exasperated the king by flirting with the more handsome of his commanders; it was rumored that she made love with her uncle, the prince of Antioch, and that she had even threatened

to elope with the twelve-year-old Saladin—who was already, she declared, more of a man than her mournful, mealy-mouth husband.

Soon after returning home to France, Louis decided that he could endure this virago of a wife no longer. It was not only that her behavior toward him had become exasperating and humiliating, although that was undeniably so: she had borne him two daughters but no son, and his kingdom must have an heir. Eleanor, it turned out, was not in the least averse to leaving Louis. She was duchess of Aquitaine in her own right, and she knew that she would have no difficulty in finding a new—and more virile—husband. To the consternation of Louis, who hoped Aquitaine would descend to their daughters, Eleanor accepted the proposal of Henry of Normandy, who had, upon his father's recent death in a jousting tournament, become count of Anjou as well.

Eleanor and Henry II were married at Whitsuntide in 1152, thus bringing together domains that stretched from the English Channel to the Pyrenees. Two years later Henry pushed these frontiers even farther north when his uncle, King Stephen of England, died without a male heir and Henry was acclaimed his successor and crowned, as Henry II, in Westminster Abbey.

The Loire ran through the very heart of Henry's by then vast holdings, and he was often seen in one or another of the castles along the river's banks, many of them built by his ancestor Fulk the Black, whose character in so many ways resembled his own. Eleanor, as vigorous and vivacious as ever, followed him about, remaining behind only when

she was too advanced in pregnancy to travel in safety. She had at least eight children by Henry, the last of them when she was forty-five. By then it was clear that she and her husband, who was eleven years younger than she, did not much enjoy each other's company anymore. Restless, never tired, and never satisfied, looking always for new excitements and new fields to conquer, Henry took to bed a variety of other, younger women and lost interest in his wife. Eleanor, having made up her mind to live apart from him, moved south to the warm lands of Aquitaine she loved so well; and in Poitou her taste for intrigue was indulged by visits from her sons, whom she encouraged to revolt against their father.

They needed little encouragement, as it happened, for none felt satisfied with the inheritance planned for him. Henry, the eldest of the four, was destined to inherit England, Normandy, and the Loire country of Anjou and Touraine. Richard, the second son and his mother's favorite, was promised her huge duchy of Aquitaine. Geoffrey, the third son, was to rule Brittany, of which his father claimed to be overlord, the duke of Brittany's daughter having been promised as Geoffrey's bride. It was hoped that John, the youngest, would settle for a religious life. To that end he had been entrusted to the monks of the abbey at Fontevrault, by the waters of the Loire, where it was hoped that he might become a novice and perhaps eventually a prince of the church. Having nothing better to offer John, his father nicknamed him Lackland; it was a sobriquet that, as he grew to manhood, John determined to prove inappropriate.

In time Henry came to recognize that his youngest son had no inclination toward a religious life, and he attempted to provide for John by marrying him to a daughter of the count of Maurienne, who possessed great fiefs in northern Italy, and by giving him, as wedding presents, three castles in the central Loire valley. These were Loudon, later demolished by Cardinal Richelieu; Mirebeau, built on a limestone escarpment honeycombed by caves that served the local peasants as subterranean dwellings; and Chinon, perhaps the most famous of all Loire castles, its three strongholds and deep moats now associated most closely with Joan of Arc. Henry's generosity may have placated John but it infuriated his eldest son, Henry, who insisted that Loudon, Mirebeau, and Chinon were part of his own inheritance. Determined to retain them, he sought the help of King Louis VII of France. Louis had private motives for coming to Prince Henry's aid, but he also had a ready-made public excuse: Prince Henry had recently married his daughter Margaret, a child of his second marriage. This made his ex-wife's son his son-in-law as well.

Not for the first time the sons of Henry and Eleanor quarreled with each other. As children they had fought continuously, and when attempts had been made to separate them they had protested that they could not help themselves—they were bound to act like devils, for the blood of Satan himself ran through their veins. "It is our proper nature to fight each other," said Prince Geoffrey, who now joined Prince Henry in revolt. "It is planted in us by our inheritance from our ancestors. None of us can love

In Celtic, Chinon means "the white one"—and although the appellation is accurate when applied to the high, sun-bleached walls of this ancient redoubt, it does belie the castle's dark history. It was at Chinon that Henry II died in 1189, abandoned by his family. And, according to popular tradition, it was to Chinon that Henry's son and successor, Richard I, was brought to die a decade later of blood poisoning from a battle wound.

His courage was undeniable, his looks prepossessing, and his exploits the stuff of legend. Small wonder, then, that Richard the Lion-Hearted should belong as much to literature as he does to history. It is almost possible to imagine that the Richard we know from the novels of Sir Walter Scott could wrestle with the beast whose name is part of his sobriquet—as Richard Coeur de Lion is seen to do in this detail from a twelfth-century manuscript.

the other. Brother must always strive against brother, and son against father."

Making the most of these family dissensions, Louis VII encouraged the barons in his territories to support the sons against their father and was delighted to see the young princes squabbling among themselves. Prince Henry died of dysentery in 1183, and this led to a further outburst of quarreling since Richard refused to take over his brother's inheritance, thus releasing Aquitaine for John. Geoffrey thereupon sided with John against Richard, while their father, in an effort to separate them, sent John to rule on his behalf in Ireland. But John did not consider Ireland worth taking seriously and soon came back to the Loire.

John returned to find that his brother Geoffrey had been killed in a tournament and that a new king, Philip II, was on the throne of France. King Philip was a cunning man, hard, unscrupulous, and capable, hiding his true nature behind a mask of gregariousness and cheerful good nature. Determined to take over the Loire valley and all the other Angevin dominions from his constantly bickering neighbors, he sought to provide them with additional grounds for dissent. He had a half sister, Alice, who had been betrothed to Prince Richard and had been entrusted to the care of her future father-in-law, Henry II, until the time came for her to marry. It was rumored that King Henry, overwhelmed by lust, had seduced this young girl, had made her his mistress, and had even had a child by her, an infant that had either died or been disposed of. King Philip made the most of these stories, broadcasting his belief that King

Henry would never let his son marry Princess Alice now and that he intended to disinherit Richard.

Inclined to believe that all this was so, Richard demanded that his father formally recognize him as his heir; he was, after all, the eldest surviving son. His demand was immediately supported by the French king, which so antagonized Henry that he curtly refused to make any such declaration. So war broke out again, with Prince John joining his brother against his father—who, worn out by his exertions to control his meddlesome offspring, was not expected to live much longer. The expectation was well justified. The strain of fighting this last campaign was too much for Henry. Harried from one stronghold to another, he finally arrived at Chinon on the Loire in June 1189. He died there at the beginning of the following month and was buried a few miles away in the abbey church of Fontevrault.

At long last Richard succeeded to the English throne as Richard I. He had little of his father's administrative ability but all of his immense energy and courage. Tall, athletic, and handsome, with extremely long arms and legs, Richard seemed the very epitome of the heroic medieval knight who scorns ease and comfort to fight the Infidel under the banner of the Cross. In fact, the new king was not quite such a paragon. Although no one could deny Richard's extraordinary bravery in battle—courageousness that earned him the nickname Lion-Hearted—there was much else in the character of this restless, commanding homosexual of savage temper and churlish arrogance that elicited fear and distaste rather than affection and respect.

Preoccupied with dreams of glory in the Holy Land, Richard made preparations to join the great crusade against Saladin even before his coronation, mustering ships, enlisting troops, and raising money by selling castles, offices, towns, privileges, and anything else for which buyers could be found. Then, after making what arrangements he could for the preservation of his inheritance, Richard set sail for the Near East—reassured that since King Philip of France was coming with him, his Continental possessions were, for the moment at least, secure from serious attack. Richard soon quarreled with Philip, whom he had already annoyed by refusing to marry Princess Alice, and the French king promptly returned home, where he fell to intriguing with Richard's brother John.

On Richard's return to the Loire valley, however, his enemies lost their nerve. One particular castellan who had earlier declared his support for Prince John was said to have actually died of fright, so awesome was the reputation for military skill and ruthlessness that Richard the Lion-Hearted had earned in Palestine. Other rebels ran for cover. John himself, kneeling submissively at his older brother's feet and trembling in abject terror, was forgiven with the contemptuous words, "Think no more of it, John. You are only a child." And John—who was, in fact, twenty-seven at the time—was so relieved to be let off lightly that he readily agreed to recover Normandy for Richard while the king himself rode off to deal with the insurgents in the central Loire.

News of Richard's approach struck terror throughout the valley. Several castles surrendered

immediately, and the garrisons of those that did not lived to regret their folly. The rebels holding Loches, whose superb natural defenses had been greatly strengthened by Henry II, deemed their fortifications impregnable and declined to open their gates when instructed to do so by the king's heralds. But Richard's skill in detecting a weak spot in a defense system—acquired through years of study of Saracen castles in the Holy Land—amounted to genius: his sudden attack on the most vulnerable point in Loches's fortifications came as a total surprise to its defenders, and within three hours the castle was his again—a triumph Richard's enemies attributed to the miraculous intervention of the demon from whom he was said to be descended.

A man who took such risks as Richard did could not always expect to be so fortunate, as the seemingly invincible king was to discover at Chalus. Following the recapture of Loches, Richard led his army off to lay siege to this castle, whose lord he accused of cheating him and whose means of defense he considered so paltry that he did not even trouble to put on his armor. During the first hours of the siege he caught sight of a crossbowman taking careful aim at him before letting loose a bolt—and, with characteristic bravado, he shouted out congratulations to the bowman on his well-aimed shot before leaping out of its path. The king moved a fraction of a second too late, however: the bolt struck him in the shoulder, and its point buried itself deep in his flesh. Dismissing the wound as of no consequence, Richard carried on with the siege operations until, almost a fortnight later, the castle was finally taken.

By then the wound was gangrenous, and the king was dying of blood poisoning, to which he succumbed on the evening of April 6, 1199. After his legendary heart had been excised and sent separately to Rouen for interment in the great cathedral there, Richard's remains were buried, as he himself had specifically requested, at his father's feet in the abbey church of Fontevrault.

Richard the Lion-Hearted, dead at forty-two, bequeathed his Angevin inheritance to his brother John, who lost no time in galloping down from Brittany to Chinon to secure his new holdings. But now that the much-feared Richard was dead, few thought that John would be able to retain control of his family's vast holdings—and such thoughts made local lords bold.

John was far from being the craven and monstrous creature of popular legend, however. He was intelligent and hard-working as well as self-indulgent, determined as well as irreverent, a capable administrator, and a clever, though cautious, military commander. He was also suspicious, untrustworthy, tyrannical, and impatient—in this, popular legend was not wrong. Often violent and sometimes exceedingly cruel, he was widely known for his fits of uncontrollable temper, terrifying even in a member of Satan's brood. During these rages he was reported to roll about the floor, clawing at the air and gnawing sticks and straw, his face mottled with livid patches. This combination of madness and method, of utter unpredictability and shrewd judgment, made him a far more formidable opponent than the Angevin aristocracy had taken him for.

From the very outset of his reign John found himself surrounded by enemies. No sooner had he returned to the central Loire than his sister-in-law Constance, the widow of his brother Geoffrey, put her twelve-year-old son Arthur under the protection of the king of France and raised a Breton army to claim the Angevin inheritance on the boy's behalf. This army marched down the Loire to Angers and seized the town in Arthur's name. Meanwhile, King Philip of France led an army through Maine. John suddenly found it prudent to retire to Normandy and thence take ship for England, where he was crowned in Westminster Abbey on May 25.

The news that followed John to England from France was profoundly disturbing. Normandy remained faithful; and his mother, still strong at seventy-seven, held Aquitaine. Between Normandy and Aquitaine, however, lay the strategically important valley of the Loire. And on the Loire, though a few castles and fortified towns declared their support for him, the Bretons were well-established between Angers and Saumur, while King Philip's troops had now seized control of Tours and Blois.

John understood well enough that if he remained much longer in England his whole Continental inheritance might soon be lost. Thus, scarcely more than a fortnight after his coronation, he returned to Normandy with a large army, intending to gather additional forces in the duchy before marching south. Disregarding the threat of a French army that had invaded Normandy along both banks of the Seine and rejecting demands to hand over Anjou, Maine, and Touraine to his nephew Arthur of Brittany, John advanced toward the Loire. Alarmed by news of his approach, William des Roches—the most influential of those barons in Anjou who had declared their support of Arthur—changed sides on condition that he be left undisturbed in possession of his lands and agreed to act as intermediary between King John and the Bretons. Deserted by their principal ally, Arthur and his mother submitted to John at Le Mans, and shortly thereafter King Philip also agreed to make peace with him. On May 22, 1200, a treaty was signed at Le Goulet. It left John in possession of virtually all the lands that Richard the Lion-Hearted had bequeathed to him in exchange for his acknowledging Philip his rightful overlord.

Although many of his critics now called him "Softsword" for having so quickly come to terms with Philip, John could congratulate himself on having survived the first military campaign of his reign without disgrace or significant loss of territory. To be recognized by the king of France as the rightful heir to the Angevin inheritance was of limited benefit to John, however, if his claims were not also recognized by the lords of the Loire. John therefore decided, in the summer of 1200, to make a tour of his dominions, taking with him a very large and exceedingly intimidating army.

He traveled through Normandy and Maine, then up the Loire from castle to castle, grandly accepting the homage and dutiful respects of his vassals and demanding hostages from towns and families whom he felt were untrustworthy. From the Loire valley he marched south into the duchy of Aquitaine, where his aged mother declared him to be her heir. And there, having had his first, childless marriage pronounced invalid by a clutch of subservient bishops, he married Isabelle, the twelve-year-old daughter of Count Aymer of Angoulême. It was a politically advantageous match, but it aroused the fury of Hugh le Brun, the powerful lord of Lusignan and count of La Marche to whom Isabelle had originally been betrothed. The Lusignans accordingly rose in revolt against John, appealing to King Philip to help them in their fight against the interloper from beyond the Loire.

Writing to John as his overlord in France, Philip summoned him to appear before a court of French barons in Paris. John declined to attend the court, whereupon the barons declared that his possessions in Aquitaine and Anjou were all forfeited fiefs. At the same time it was announced that John's nephew, Arthur of Brittany, was now the rightful ruler of these territories and that King Philip himself would take possession of Normandy. Having delivered himself of these judgments, Philip led his army into Brittany while Arthur marched on the Loire.

John's reaction was firm and resolute. As soon as sufficient mercenaries had been collected in Normandy, he hurried south through Maine and Anjou and crossed the Loire at Chinon. Covering eighty miles in two days and collecting William des Roches on the way, he arrived on the night of July 31, 1201, at Mirebeau. There Arthur of Brittany's forces were holding Queen Eleanor captive in the castle keep. Early the following morning John's army, under the direction of his ally des Roches, who knew Mirebeau and its limestone mount well, laid siege to the castle.

Shortly after dawn the king's troops stormed through Mirebeau's gates, released Eleanor, and captured Hugh le Brun and Arthur of Brittany.

Arthur's subsequent fate was recorded in graphic detail by William de Brionze, one of John's commanders at Mirebeau:

> After King John had kept Arthur in captivity for some time in the castle of Rouen—after dinner on the Thursday before Easter, when the king was drunk and possessed by a devilish rage—he slew him with his own hand and, tying a heavy stone to the body, cast it into the river.

This appalling murder was to have dreadful consequences for the assassin, whose brilliant victory at Mirebeau was of no avail. For even before they heard of the death of their young hero an army of Bretons, enraged by the mere fact of Arthur's humiliating captivity at Rouen, had swept down the Loire valley and taken Angers. The central valley east of Angers now fell largely into the hands of rebels led by William des Roches, whose inability to conceal his disgust at King John's high-handed methods had led to his dismissal as the king's seneschal in Anjou. Repulsed and rejected, des Roches became, once more, an ally of the king of France.

To deal with these renewed threats to his Angevin inheritance, John rode in haste to the central Loire—where he soon discovered that the situation was more grave than he had dared to imagine. He was obliged to return to Normandy, where he sought to raise another, larger army to confront the Bretons and des Roches. Before he was able to do so, word reached him that his wife, Queen Isabelle, was surrounded by rebels at Chinon. He departed immediately with a small band of mercenaries, bent on rescuing her; but he had scarcely crossed into Maine when he learned of the defection of the count of Alençon, at whose castle he had been entertained only two nights earlier. Utterly discouraged, John pulled up at Le Mans, that favorite city of his father, Henry II, and took temporary refuge in the great keep built by William the Conqueror. Sending his mercenaries on to Chinon without him, John sulked about the Norman keep, giving vent to outbursts of the most horrifying rage.

The coming of spring found King John still at Le Mans—and his queen still encircled at Chinon. This left the French king and his allies free to march without hindrance into the central Loire valley from their base at Orléans, to sail downstream to Saumur, and thence to travel overland to join the Poitevin rebels in their attacks on castles in Aquitaine.

As long as Eleanor was alive, King Philip dared not launch a full-scale attack on her duchy. But on April 1, 1204, at the age of eighty-two, the doughty queen died. Philip waited until Eleanor had been buried alongside her husband and two of her sons at Fontevrault, then marched through Anjou, joined forces with William des Roches, and invaded Poitou with a large army of mercenaries. Normandy had already fallen; and soon the whole of Poitou was also in the French king's hands. Preferring to owe allegiance to a weak king in faraway England than a powerful one in France, the barons farther south in

Like Loches, Saumur castle was considered a linchpin of the Loire valley defense system, and consequently the Plantagenets and their Capetian rivals vied to possess the mighty fortress throughout the late twelfth and early thirteenth centuries. Set, like Blois, on a sheer promontory overlooking the Loire, this high-walled keep was part of Henry II's dowry from Eleanor of Aquitaine. The present structure, which dates from the late 1300's, when it was erected at the behest of the same Louis of Anjou who commissioned the Angers tapestries, is a fine example of the transition from medieval military to Renaissance architecture. An equine museum (right), housed on the castle's second floor, contains a renowned collection of saddles, bridles, spurs and other trap— and such curiosities as the complete skeleton of Flying Fox, winner of the 1899 English Derby.

Angoulême held out—and this gave John hope that if he mounted a determined invasion of southwestern France all might yet be saved.

Throughout the late spring of 1205, urgent preparations were made in England—to which John had prudently withdrawn as matters went from bad to worse in the central Loire—for this momentous expedition. Huge stores of equipment and provisions were collected; large numbers of troops were mustered; immense sums of money were spent. But as the time for sailing drew near, John's barons showed themselves to be less and less keen to venture abroad with him. Faced with their collective reluctance, the king concluded that he would have to cancel the expedition altogether. Meanwhile, resistance in John's last remaining strongholds in the Loire valley collapsed. At Easter the garrison at Chinon, forced to abandon the castle after an eight-month siege, came out fighting—only to be overwhelmed by King Philip's mercenaries. Then, in the summer of 1205, Loches fell. This reversal was a particularly significant one, for the enormous rectangular bastion had symbolic as well as strategic importance. Loches, which stood on a high promontory 121 feet about the Loire, was widely regarded as the best fortified—and therefore least vulnerable—of Loire valley castles. Continuously reinforced throughout the twelfth and thirteenth centuries, it was thought to be impregnable—and its surrender marked the end of all resistance to King Philip in the valley of the Loire.

There were, at this time, one or two strongholds in the south that were still holding out in John's name. In a last, desperate effort to regain some part of what he had lost, John now persuaded a number of his barons to join him in the long-delayed invasion. He landed in the harbor of La Rochelle at the beginning of June 1206, and although his army was far from strong he marched boldly into Aquitaine, capturing Montauban and gathering sufficient support in the course of his successful raids into Poitou to encourage him once more to advance north into the Loire valley. His forces came down to the riverbank at Port Alaschert, where, so a chronicler recorded, "he made the sign of the Cross over the waters with his hand, and, trusting to the help of God, forded the river with all his host, which is a marvelous thing to tell and such was never heard of in our time."

In September, John entered Angers in triumph and remained there for a week. Then he progressed northward through Anjou as far as the border with Maine before returning across the Loire near Chinon and south again to Poitou. It was a highly effective demonstration; King Philip, duly impressed, agreed to a truce that recognized John's right to hold onto the possessions he had regained. It was to be another six years, however, before John felt his position in England to be strong enough for him to venture a campaign against Philip with an army capable of defeating the French king in open battle—and even then John was compelled to leave behind him a country seething with discontent.

After some preliminary forays in Aquitaine, during which he gathered reinforcements from various loyal barons in Poitou, John advanced north across

57

the Loire in June 1214, seized Ancenis on the Breton border, and then, after a short, vicious battle by the bridge at Nantes, captured that city. Stunned and alarmed by King John's unexpected victory at Nantes, the citizens of Angers opened their gates to him—admitting John and his retinue to the ancient capital of the Plantagenets, the capital from which he had been excluded for such a long time.

Heartened by these early successes, John rode out from Angers to subdue William des Roches—who, as King Philip's senechal, had built himself a large new castle near Angers at Roche-du-Maine. But then, just as the castle seemed on the verge of collapse after a fortnight's battering by siege engines—and when, against all odds, King John seemed on the verge of bringing the whole of Anjou once again under his control—a French army came to des Roches' assistance under the command of King Philip's twenty-six-year-old son, Louis. At Louis' approach, the Poitevin barons lost their nerve and rode for home, taking their knights and retainers with them. Cursing them in paroxysms of rage, John withdrew to La Rochelle. A month later John's bastard half brother, William, earl of Salisbury, together with all the allies that he had been able to muster, was defeated by King Philip at Bouvines in the morasses of Flanders. John's last hopes of ever regaining his family's great inheritance were dashed. He sailed for England—there to face insurrection, civil war, Runnymede, Magna Charta, and death—and left the Loire to his enemies.

John's pretty, mischievous young widow, Isabelle, who had been able to escape Chinon and rejoin her husband in England during a temporary cessation of hostilities in the central Loire—only to be imprisoned at Gloucester by her increasingly paranoid husband for her infidelities, real and imagined—returned to France after his death in 1216. Four years later she married her former suitor, Hugh le Brun, lord of Lusigan and count of La Marche. Isabelle lived on for another twenty-six years and died at Fontevrault—where, having separated from le Brun and quarreled with all her friends, she had sought the protection of the nuns of the abbey. She was buried there in 1246, in a simple grave in the cemetery adjoining a house reserved for the use of noblewomen who had retreated from the outside world for one reason or another.

Eight years later her elder son, by then King Henry III of England, visited this grave, the resting place of a mother he had scarcely known. So moved was Henry by its insignificance that he had Isabelle's remains moved inside the abbey church. This imposing structure, 92 yards in length and covered with pendentive cupolas, is dominated by an echoing nave that dates from the twelfth century. At its far end are the tombs of the Plantagenets. Isabelle's tomb has not survived, although the early thirteenth-century polychrome effigy that Henry III had placed over his mother's crypt can still be seen. Beside it are effigies of Isabelle's mother-in-law, Eleanor of Aquitaine; of Eleanor's husband Henry II; and of their second son, Richard I—moving reminders that this lovely abbey on the Loire once lay within the realms of the Plantagenet kings of England, who were also counts of Anjou.

IV

The Road to Orléans

Deeply mortified by the loss of their possessions in the rich Loire valley, King John's descendants kept a wary watch for opportunities to regain them. Several ill-managed expeditions to France were made during the long reign of the incompetent Henry III, but troubles at home as well as in Scotland and Wales prevented Henry's more talented son, Edward I, from challenging the claims of his young cousin Philip the Fair, king of France. And Edward's son, the extravagant, frivolous, and emotionally unstable Edward II, had neither the means nor the will to carry out the great enterprises he talked about so grandiosely in his cups. Thus, it was left to Edward III to regain for his family the great Angevin inheritance of his ancestors.

Edward III was certainly a man well-suited to the task he set himself. By turns vengeful and forgiving, at once self-indulgent and flamboyantly pious, he was also handsome, brave, ambitious, of great physical strength and limitless energy. His opportunity to reassert his family's claims in France came in 1342, with the death of the duke of Brittany and the subsequent battle for the succession to the duchy between the duke's younger brother, John de Montfort, and his son-in-law, Charles of Blois. King Philip VI of France, in support of Charles of Blois, invaded Brittany and captured de Montfort. Assuming the role of de Montfort's champion, Edward dispatched an expeditionary force to rescue the claimant's wife, whom the French were besieging at Hennebont.

The English were in a confident mood. Two years earlier they had won an overwhelming naval victory against the French at Sluys, where a large part of the

French fleet had been destroyed. That battle had also afforded a convincing demonstration of the extraordinary prowess of the English archers, whose bows were "thicker and longer than those used by other nations, just as their bodies [were] stronger than other people's." This confidence was amply justified. At Morlaix in Brittany in 1342, as at Sluys in 1340, the English archers proved their incomparable worth by defeating an enemy force far larger than their own. Taking advantage of this victory, King Edward himself landed in Brittany, advanced south to occupy Vannes, and sent a fighting patrol even farther south to take the city of Nantes.

Determined to throw the invaders out of France before they made any further dangerous inroads into his territories, King Philip assembled a huge army at Angers and marched down the Loire to the relief of Nantes. Unable to withstand the onslaught of so vast a host and running out of supplies, Edward was glad to accept a truce and to agree that Charles of Blois could remain in possession of those parts of Brittany he then occupied, provided John de Montfort could retain the south and west. From the English point of view it was a satisfactory opening—to a war that was to last for a hundred years.

The Loire valley was untroubled by fighting during the early campaigns of this war, in which the English successes were achieved in southern France, in Normandy at Crécy, where Philip VI was overwhelmed, and in Brittany at La Roche-Derrien, where Charles of Blois was taken prisoner. But in October 1355, King Edward's young son—the dashing Prince of Wales, known as "the Black Prince"

because of his black armor—landed at Bordeaux and set out with five thousand men from England and Gascony on a *grande chevauchée,* looting and burning buildings, stores, and crops until he had laid waste the rich countryside of southwestern France as far as Narbonne, only ten miles from the shores of the Mediterranean. The next summer the Black Prince crossed the Dordogne with an even larger force and marched toward the Loire, ravaging the villages and towns of Touraine on his way.

The Black Prince's army advanced about ten miles a day; and at the beginning of September he came up to the Loire at Amboise. Since all the bridges around Amboise had either been broken down or were strongly held by the French, he turned west and, in pouring rain, advanced downstream as far as Tours. The river was now in flood; and the Black Prince decided to encamp outside the town, sending out foraging parties to bring in supplies and raiding parties to attack the nearby castles. Fearing that the English and Gascons would soon be across the Loire, John II, Philip's successor as king of France, quickly came to terms with the rebels in Normandy with whom he had been fighting and led an army south. He sent advance parties across the Loire, hoping to cross it himself before the season was much further advanced. But the Black Prince evaded him. He withdrew from Tours into Poitou, drawing King John after him. At Poitiers, on September 19, 1356, toward the end of a savage day's fighting in which the French appeared to have gained the upper hand, "fortune turned her giddy wheel, and the Prince of Wales penetrated the ranks of the enemy

and, like a lion with noble wrath, spared the lowly and put down the mighty and took the King of France prisoner," a contemporary historian reported.

King John was not the only prisoner. Also taken that day were one of his sons, an archbishop, five viscounts, thirteen counts, over twenty barons, and nearly two thousand knights. Two dukes lay dead on the field as well as 2,500 other knights. When the English returned home, there was scarcely a woman in the whole island, so it was said, who was not given a jewel or ornament, a goblet or a piece of fine cloth, some precious piece of plunder brought home from the triumphant campaign that had ended on the blood-spattered field of Poitiers.

As England rejoiced, France was plunged into turmoil. While her king languished in captivity, unable to raise the immense ransom demanded for his release, the dauphin, an inexperienced youth of eighteen, was faced with rebellion. Entire provinces were abandoned to the mercy of marauding gangs of brigands composed largely of disbanded mercenaries. The Loire valley was plundered from end to end by a peculiarly savage band led by a Welshman, John Griffith, whose very name struck terror into the heart of every peasant between Angers and Saumur. In these dreadful times men "made huts in the woods, there eating their bread in fear, sadness and grief" according to a fourteenth-century historian who added that the dead were "left lying about the villages and hamlets"; "vines were not pruned or kept from rotting by the labours of man's hands; the fields were not sown or ploughed, there were no cattle or fowls in the fields. The pleasant sound of

bells was heard, not as a summons to divine worship but in order that men might seek out hiding places."

Into this ravaged country, King Edward prepared once more to march. He was now demanding the cession of Anjou, Maine, and Touraine as well as Poitou and Normandy. To enforce his demand, he assembled vast amounts of stores and planned his invasion in such detail that even leather coracles were brought down from the Severn to the south coast of England so that during Lent the army would be able to eat fish supplied by the Loire and the other rivers of France.

In October 1359 there landed at Calais the advance guard of an army described as being the greatest and best ordered that ever "departed out of England." Through devastated country in torrential rain the huge host advanced south toward the Loire. Behind the king's men-at-arms and archers trundled "all the carriages, a procession two leagues in length, more than five thousand wagons and carts, every cart with at least four good horses brought out of England, making provision for the host with all things necessary. Then after came the Prince of Wales's squadrons and those of his brothers, wherein were two thousand spears nobly horsed and richly caparisoned . . . and five hundred varlets with mattocks and axes to make even the ways of the carriages to pass."

Yet this great army, lusting for battle, could find no one to fight. Rather than face the English archers and cavalry at another Poitiers, the French had been ordered to offer the invaders no resistance in the field, to shut themselves up behind fortified walls,

and to wait. It was a highly effective strategy. For most of two bitterly cold months the English army laid siege to Reims, where Edward had sworn to have himself crowned king of France. But the gates of Reims stayed closed, and no relieving army appeared to offer battle. Before the end of January, Edward was obliged to move across the Loire to the less cold lands of Burgundy, where he hoped to find grazing for his horses when the warm weather came.

It was a long, hard winter, and many weeks passed before the English army could move north again. When they could it was April, but even so there was no fodder for the horses in the countryside around Paris, where a French garrison ignored the repeated challenges of English heralds. Thus, Edward was obliged once more to withdraw to the Loire; and on Monday, April 13, a dark day of mist and hail so cold that many soldiers froze to death in their saddles, the retreat began. By the end of the month it was still as cold as ever; and one terrible day, when the Loire was almost in sight, such a "tempest of thunder, lightning and hail" broke over the army's head "that it seemed the world should have ended." As huge hailstones fell from the clouds, lightning struck at the armor of the knights, killing more of them—so chroniclers reported—than had died on the fields of Crécy and Poitiers.

The loss of so many men did not deter the English leaders from their attempt to draw the French out from behind their fortress walls into open battle. "Certain knights in the retinue of the Duke of Lancaster," reported one chronicler, "disguising themselves as brigands or pillaging soldiers without

Comment le roy Jehan fut
pris en la bataille de poitiers
et ses gens mors et desconfiz

Quant le prince de galles
vit que combatre se
convenoit et que le

lances, rode in pretended disarray in order to give the enemy spirit and courage to fight them. Some . . . overdid their performance to such an extent . . . that they came to grief and were captured."

Tempted and taunted as they were, the French wisely declined to be provoked; and ultimately King Edward was obliged to come to terms. Discussions between the two sides were opened at the beginning of May 1360, and a treaty was signed at the village of Brétigny. By this treaty Edward was recognized as ruler of all Aquitaine as well as Calais and Ponthieu and was to hold these territories entirely in his own right, free from the suzerainty of the French king. He was also to receive the full amount demanded for King John's ransom. But in return he was to renounce his claim to Normandy and Brittany, Anjou, Maine, and Touraine: the whole of the Loire was to become incontestably French. And so it might well have remained had not delays and prevarications prevented the treaty's clauses dealing with mutual renunciations of sovereignty from being ratified. As it was, these vital matters were left in dispute; and the English king chose to consider that his claim to sovereignty over all France had been postponed rather than abandoned.

For the moment, though, there was little that Edward could do to press his claim. In 1364 King John died and was succeeded by the young, wily, and astute dauphin as Charles V. King Charles was a scholar rather than a warrior: he had not fought in a battle since Poitiers and was never to fight in the field again. But frail and reticent as he appeared, no one who knew him well could mistake the strength of his character and the shrewdness of his judgment. He was one of the first to recognize the military acumen of the tough, squat, ill-mannered, and ill-featured Breton soldier Bertrand du Guesclin, and he had no hesitation in appointing him to the supreme command of the French army. It was a fateful choice. No English commander could rival du Guesclin's skill and stolid patience. And as castles were strengthened and districts still loyal to the king of England were gradually subdued one after the other, English power in France began to crumble.

Because du Guesclin declined to expose his army to the possibility of defeat, no pitched battles were fought; and his Fabian tactics finally wore out the English. The Black Prince, frustrated, embittered, and ill, gave up Aquitaine to his brother John of Gaunt and went home to die. John, in turn, married the eldest daughter of Don Pedro of Castile and went off to try his fortune in Spain. King Edward III, in senile devotion to a grasping mistress, seemed scarcely aware that his empire was collapsing around him. In 1373, in a final effort to regain an authority long since lost, an English army marched from Calais across the Loire to Bordeaux, losing thousands of horses in the bitterly cold winter nights. But Charles V and du Guesclin let the army pass unmolested, allowing it to waste its strength to little purpose. And by the beginning of the next year the English had been driven back to Calais and to strips of land around Bordeaux and the harbors of Brittany. As the fourteenth century ended, the war degenerated into little more than a series of indecisive raids and skirmishes.

But fortune's wheel was already turning again. On Passion Sunday of 1413, Edward III's great-grandson was crowned as Henry V in Westminster Abbey. He had been a foppish, dissolute youth; now, at twenty-five, he was a grave, thoughtful, and determined man. Looking at his tightly compressed lips and at the set of his head, shaved at the back and sides as the heads of soldiers were, men could find grounds for hope that a new age was dawning. They were not to be disappointed. The coronation ceremony was scarcely over when Henry formally revived the claims of his ancestors to their lost lands in France. Soon afterward he declared himself king of France by right of succession from his great-great-grandmother Isabella, daughter of Philip IV.

The declaration was well-timed. Charles V had died in 1380; and his successor as king of France, Charles VI, was prematurely old at forty-four. Plagued by a detested wife who flaunted her lovers in his face, Charles was intermittently mad, one of his convictions being that he was made of glass and that if people came too near him he would break. Moreover, Charles's domains were being torn apart by rivalries and jealousies. Yet, favorable as the time was for an invasion of France, no one could possibly have foreseen the astonishing success of Henry V's campaign, which ended on October 25, 1415, at Agincourt. There, in a pitched battle that lasted barely three hours, a depleted and exhausted force of some five thousand Englishmen, mostly archers, routed a French army four or five times its size and lost no more than a hundred men to the enemy's seven thousand to ten thousand dead.

The consequences of Agincourt were certainly far-reaching. The whole Christian world was impressed; and Henry was able to return to France, after huge ransoms had been exacted for his prisoners, a feared and respected conqueror. By 1419 he had conquered all Normandy; and in the following year, by the Treaty of Troyes, he was made heir and regent of France, marrying Charles VI's daughter Catherine and dispossessing Charles's son, the dauphin. In 1422, however, having brought almost the whole of the country to the north of the Loire under his control, Henry's health broke down and at the age of thirty-four he died at Vincennes. He was succeeded by his infant son, Henry VI.

Some three years later a young girl in the village of Domremy in Lorraine, while in her father's garden at midday, was suddenly terrified by a strange voice speaking to her "on her right side, in the direction of the church." Joan of Arc was then thirteen years old, an obedient, well-behaved, kindly girl, rather small for her age but very strong. Without being pretty, she had a pleasant, dark-skinned country girl's face with black hair, eyes spaced far apart, and a red birthmark behind her left ear. Apart from a piety so pronounced that other children in the village teased her about it, there was nothing unusual about her—until she heard that frightening voice speaking to her from the church.

Joan soon outgrew her fear, having identified the speaker as the Archangel Michael, who then manifested himself before her and began transmitting messages to her. At first her instructions were merely to be a good girl, which she was already; then she

"Harry the King" he calls himself in Shakespeare's drama Henry V, *and in this contemporary portrait the young English monarch looks every inch the "plain soldier" of that play. The soldierly skills of this fellow of plain and uncoined constancy were to serve the English cause well on October 25, 1415. Encountering a substantially larger French force at Agincourt, King Harry and his troops were to deal their longtime enemies a disastrous defeat—and to recapture, albeit only temporarily, much of the northern Loire valley. This pivotal battle, which is ostensibly depicted in the manuscript detail at left, actually occurred on a narrow plain between two woods—where English archers easily outflanked their cumbersomely armored rivals and slaughtered as many as 10,000 of them in a single afternoon.*

was told that she must go to the aid of the French king. Finally she learned that it was God's will that she should go to Orléans, which was being besieged by the English; relieve the city; take the dauphin—who, despite the Treaty of Troyes, was widely recognized in France as Charles VII—to be crowned at Reims; and drive the English out of the country.

Charles VII had already been crowned at Poitiers. But it was the opinion of many pious people that no monarch could consider himself the true ruler of France until he had been anointed with the sacred oil that a dove from heaven had brought down for the consecration of King Clovis and which was preserved in a reliquary, miraculously replenished after each coronation, behind the great altar in Reims Cathedral. Joan shared the view of the pious and seemed to have had no doubt that it was God's will that she should fight the English so as to be able to take the king to Reims in triumph. But her father, a solid, respectable, down-to-earth farmer, one of the leading men in the village, considered her ridiculous. If she thought she was going off to the wars like a common harlot, she was very much mistaken; he would have her trussed up in a sack and thrown into the millpond.

Joan would not be dissuaded. Although she continued to help her mother in the small, gray stone house where she had been born, the voices grew more and more insistent and she could not ignore them. She felt compelled to go to the nearby town of Vaucouleurs, demand to see the governor, and persuade him to recommend her to the king—to whom she would then convey the messages she had received from God. She actually managed to obtain a hearing from the governor, who listened in amazement to the village girl's story: how voices had told her to ask the governor of Vaucouleurs for an escort to take her to the king; how she was to tell the king that he must not lose heart, for God was on his side; how she herself would lead his soldiers into battle and afterward conduct him to his coronation. When Joan had finished, the astounded governor sent her packing, telling her cousin's husband, who had brought her into his presence, to take the impudent girl back to her father for a thorough whipping.

She went away but insisted on returning for another interview with the governor. He remained unconvinced of her sincerity—though he took the precaution this time of writing to the king to ask if he ought to send the girl on to Chinon. Impatient of the delay, Joan determined to set out for Chinon without further ado. Exchanging her red dress for men's clothes, she rode down toward the Loire. On her way, however, she stopped to pray at a little chapel; and there—remembering in the middle of her prayers that the voices had told her to obtain an escort—she decided it was wrong to proceed to Chinon alone. She returned to Vaucouleurs and once more went to see the governor to reiterate her demands. Now, at last, he was prepared to listen to her, for he had received a reply from Chinon instructing him to send the girl there once he had satisfied himself that she was not possessed by the devil. Having consulted a priest in the matter, the governor gave her his permission to proceed to Chinon. She dressed herself in a man's black doub-

let and hose, a dark gray cloak, black cap, and brown leather boots with spurs. Then, armed with a dagger given to her by the people of the town and a sword provided by the governor, she and her escort departed for the Loire on the evening of February 23, 1429. She was a mere seventeen years old.

The French king awaiting her at Chinon was twenty-six. A most unprepossessing, even deformed little figure, short and bald and astigmatic, with knock-knees and painfully thin legs, he was constantly beset by feelings of inadequacy. His mother declared him to be a bastard and he was, indeed, widely supposed to be the son of Charles VI's brother, the duke of Orléans. But although insecure, haunted by fears of illegitimacy, hesitant and highly superstitious, he was neither a fool nor a coward. He was concerned for the future of France and predisposed to believe that he might be chosen by God to save his people from the English. Joan's voices had assured her that the king, once in her presence, would receive a sure sign and believe in her.

She reached Chinon at midday on March 6 and took a room at an inn while waiting for arrangements to be made for her reception at court. The huge, sprawling castle towered above her. The oldest part, the Coudray keep, had been built in the tenth century. The adjoining Fort St. Georges had been started by Henry II and completed by Richard I on the lines of a Saracen castle. The middle castle was the recent work of Charles VII, who now awaited Joan in its vast, rush-strewn hall.

Joan was conducted from the inn to the castle by the count of Vendôme; and as she rode up the steep slope to the gate a man called out, "God's death! Is that the Maid? If I could have her for one night I would not return her in the same condition!"

"You swear by God's death," Joan answered him. "Yet you are very near to death yourself."

An hour later, so Joan herself as well as many others reported, the man fell into the castle moat and was drowned. By then Joan had spoken to the king. Led into the hall, where the flickering light of fifty torches shone upon the gray, tapestry-covered walls, she had immediately walked up to Charles, who was surrounded by scores of courtiers, attendants, and ladies of the royal household. "I am called Joan the Maid," she said. "And the King of Heaven sends you word by me that you will be consecrated and crowned at Reims."

Charles took her to one side to talk to her alone, to satisfy himself, so far as he could, that she was indeed sent by God and not by the devil. How could she prove herself? he asked. "Sire," she replied, "if I tell you things that are known only to God and yourself, will you believe that I am sent by the King of Heaven?. . . Do you remember that on All Saints' Day last when you were alone in your oratory in the castle of Loches you made three requests of God?" Charles did remember and confirmed that no one else knew of his prayers, not even his confessor. Joan then told him how "without spoken utterances" he had "humbly asked God if it were indeed true that he was of the blood of the noble House of France and rightful ruler of the Kingdom and, if so, that God should keep and defend him." Having listened to her in awe and astonishment, the king

Joan of Arc, the divinely-inspired peasant girl who led the army of France's uncrowned king, Charles VII, to victory over the English expeditionary forces in the central Loire valley, has been celebrated in prose and poetry, plays and paintings since her martyrdom in 1431, but this tiny marginal drawing in a fifteenth-century manuscript is the only known contemporary representation of the seventeen-year-old savior of Orléans.

OVERLEAF: *Fort St. Georges, built by Henry II, is the best-preserved of the three moated strongholds that comprise Chinon castle. The Grand Logis, as the central structure is known, is where, on March 9, 1429, Charles received Joan and heard her remarkable petition. Until April 20, the day of her departure for the beleaguered city of Orléans, Joan was housed, at the king's specific instructions, in the castle's third major structure, the centuries-old keep known as the château of Coudray.*

led her back into the hall, the expression on his ugly face revealing plainly to the company that he was convinced of her divine inspiration. He announced that she would be accepted into the royal household, would be provided with a page, and would be given lodgings at Chinon in the Coudray keep.

It was not in the king's nature, however, to remain for long untroubled by doubt; and before allowing himself to be led too far by this girl, he decided to make absolutely sure that she was all that she claimed to be. Was she, in fact, a proper female? The devil had been known to fabricate strange creatures to lead good men astray. Was she a virgin? This must be established for certain; since if she were a virgin, the devil could have had no dealings with her. And did her voices emanate from heaven?

Satisfied on all these counts, the king ordered Joan be given a suit of white armor, a black charger, and a white buckram banner—on which a Scottish artist living in Tours was asked by Joan to depict on one side a figure of Christ holding the world in his hand with angels kneeling to his right and left and, on the other side, the Virgin Mary and a shield with the arms of France. Provided also with a small battle-axe, she sent to the village of Fierbois for a sword which, she said, would be found buried behind the altar. She knew it was there because her voices had told her so. "It was found there at once," Joan said later. "It was in the ground and rusty. Upon it were five crosses. . . . As soon as it was found, the priests of the church rubbed it and the dust fell off at once without effort." It was believed to be the sword of Charles Martel, who, many cen-

turies before, had saved the Loire valley from the depredations of the Saracens.

Armed with this sword, Joan left Tours on April 24, riding along the north bank of the river at the head of a large body of troops. She headed for Blois, where supplies for the relief of Orléans were being collected and where Charles VII's army of some ten thousand men was being mustered. Also assembling at Blois were numerous monks who had abandoned the nearby abbeys at the approach of the English and who were required by Joan to rally every morning and evening around her banner to sing anthems and hymns and to receive her blessing. Most of the time, however, she spent with the soldiers, talking to their commanders and warning them all that they would win no victory unless they deserved it: prostitutes were to be banished from the ranks; swearing and blaspheming were to be punished with the most severe penalties; all sins were to be confessed to the priests who had joined Joan's train; and absolution was to be sought.

After spending four days at Blois, Joan took the army across the bridge and along the south bank of the river toward Orléans. The archers led the way, followed by the men-at-arms, six hundred wagons full of food and ammunition, four hundred head of cattle, and straggling lines of sheep and pigs. Near St. Laurent des Eaux the long convoy came to a halt for the night and Joan lay down to sleep in her armor, awaking "terribly bruised" next morning. As soon as it was light, the army moved off once more; and later that same day the head of the column reached the little town of Olivet, which stands on

rising ground two miles from Orléans. From here Joan could look down on the beleaguered city she had been sent by God to deliver.

The English, under the leadership of Henry VI's cousin, the earl of Salisbury, had arrived before the walls and begun to bombard Orléans in October of the previous year. Now, in the seventh month of the siege, the inhabitants had come close to despair. The enemy forces were not strong enough to surround the city completely or to block the passage of all supplies, but they had captured the Fort des Tourelles, a fortress commanding the bridge. They had also occupied the outlying Bastille de Loup farther upstream on the northern bank and had made large tracts of the surrounding countryside uninhabitable, thus forcing thousands of villagers to seek protection behind the walls and towers of the city, whose population had swelled from fifteen thousand to almost fifty thousand. The assaults of the English had been repulsed, yet the garrison's sallies were equally unsuccessful. Losing all confidence in their military protectors, the citizens had been driven to repose their trust in the intervention of their patron saint, Aignan, whose shrine they carried in procession around the city walls.

But now the Maid had come; and, willing to believe in miracles, the people turned to her with new confidence in their salvation. Joan crossed the Loire upstream from the city near Chécy, spent the night there, and on the evening of the next day rode into Orléans from the east through the Port de Bourgoyne, her standard fluttering before her.

Crowds flocked into the streets to welcome her, their torches flaring in the dusk, pressing close around her to look into her face. In the crush her pennon caught fire, and she spurred her way forward to trample it underfoot "as one might do that had long followed the wars," flames and sparks flying from her horse's hooves. She rode on to the Church of St. Croix to offer prayers of thanksgiving for her arrival. Then she went to stay the night at the house of the duke of Orléans' treasurer in the Rue des Talmetiers, happy in the knowledge that supplies, ammunition, and cattle had drifted safely down the river on rafts and into the city moat, hidden from the eyes of the English sentries by the tangled scrub and osiers on the midstream island known as the Île aux Boeufs.

The next day Joan walked down to the outwork nearest the Fort des Tourelles, where the English were still entrenched, and called out "in God's name" for them to retire in peace or be driven out by the sword. "Do you expect us to surrender to a *woman*?" a voice shouted back, abusing her with obscene insults. Another voice threatened, "Milkmaid! Cowherd! Harlot! When we capture you, you will be burned alive!"

The attacks on the English-held forts began on May 4; and in all of them Joan and her banner, in the thick of the fighting, were an inspiration to the French soldiers. The Bastille St. Loup fell after a fierce struggle; and, hoping that the loss of this important stronghold would induce the enemy to retire without further bloodshed, Joan once more called upon them to go back to their own country. "You men of England have no right in this Kingdom

of France," she dictated to a clerk who wrote down her words in a message that was to be tied to the head of an arrow and shot across the lines. "The King of Heaven orders and commands you by me, Joan the Maid, that you withdraw from your strongholds.... If you do not I will cause you a defeat such as will be remembered for all time."

Understandably provoked by the tone of this message, the English promptly rejected it, shouting back insults at the peasant girl who called herself a virgin yet was nothing but a harlot. Joan burst into tears at the accusation, kneeling down to pray to God for help and courage. She wept, too, when an arrow pierced her shoulder during an attack on the stone towers of the Fort des Tourelles two days later; but as the pain subsided, she recovered her spirit, returned to the attack, and helped plant scaling ladders against the walls, calling out to the English commanders, "Yield, yield to the King of Heaven! You have called me harlot. I have great pity for your souls and for the souls of your people."

All day long the fight for the Fort des Tourelles continued, until at sunset the duke of Orléans' bastard brother, the commander of the French army, ordered a withdrawal. But at Joan's urgent instigation the order was countermanded. The French surged forward once more, the Maid's banner rallying the men through the smoke. At last the fort fell; most of its defenders were slaughtered, the rest were taken prisoner. The French troops poured across the bridge, and the church bells pealed in joyful celebration of their victory. The siege of Orléans was raised.

A week later Joan rode out of Orléans in doublet and hose, a silk-lined cloak of cloth-of-gold, and a velvet hat to meet the king on the riverside road between Chinon and Tours. She galloped forward when she saw him, swept the cap from her head, and bowed low over her horse's neck. Charles told her to look up at him. She did so and he kissed her. Together they rode off to Reims at the end of June, the remaining strongholds of the English on the river having been captured and their army defeated in open battle near Patany. And Charles was crowned, as Joan had promised—she standing by his side, holding her banner.

Joan fared less well in the north: having failed to take Paris, she was captured at Compiègne and handed over to the English. With the support of the Burgundian divines of Paris University, her English captors had her burned to death as a witch in the marketplace at Rouen.

But Joan's steadfastness, confidence, and the example of her indomitable character had given strength to a cause that had almost been given up as lost—while her martyrdom wakened in France a sense of national pride that had never before existed. After her victories on the Loire, the final end of the Hundred Years' War could not be long delayed. It came in 1453 when the English had to abandon their claims to all their French possessions except Calais. Centuries were to pass before another army of English-speaking soldiers returned to the Loire valley; and when they did come, they came as friends sharing their French allies' respect for the memory of the Maid of Orléans.

LE TRESVICTORIEVX ROY DE FRANCE

CHARLES SEPTIESME DE CE NOM

74

Not for nothing was Charles VII nicknamed "the Well Served." Every bit as dull and plain as he appears in this portrait by Fouquet, Charles was indecisive to the point of paralysis, suspicious, superstitious, and sly. In the beatific, coolly assured Joan of Arc he found the serenity and self-confidence he himself lacked. He entrusted her with the impossible task of relieving Orléans (right), and in this she served her king very well indeed. The self-absorbed and vascillating monarch did not serve Joan half so well thereafter, making no effort to secure her freedom when she was captured by Burgundian troops and sold to the English after the battle of Compiègne (below). Not until 1456, twenty-five years after Joan's death at the stake, did Charles order the rehabilitation trial which annulled the proceedings of the court at Rouen that had condemned Joan to death.

Si aduint qua vnes approuche.
Les francops treffozt reaillerent.

Coment la pucelle fut prinse deuant
compiegne et vendue auw angloys.
Lozs au conflictet par surprise.

V

Princes of the Renaissance

On the western outskirts of Tours, between the Loire and its tributary the Cher, stand the remains of the château of Plessis-les-Tours. Here, toward the end of the fifteenth century, in a castle "like a frontier-station, closely guarded" and surrounded by lookout posts and crossbowmen, Charles VII's son Louis XI endured the last years of his unhappy life.

In morbid fear of death, trusting only those few men who were allowed to approach him, spending hours in consultation with his doctors and astrologers, Louis looked back in mournful regret on the errors of the past. His lot had been a hard one. As ugly as his father, with a long hooked nose and suspicious, half-closed, searching eyes, he had never known love. He had spent his childhood at the castle of Loches, rarely visited by his father. At the age of thirteen he had been married to Margaret, daughter of James I of Scotland, who regarded him with as little affection as he regarded her and far preferred the company of her father-in-law. Louis had never got on well with his father, while he positively detested Charles's mistress, the extravagant, commanding, and decorative Agnès Sorel, who presided with such grace and assurance over the French court at Chinon.

Turning his back on the courtly life, Louis chose to live among bourgeois men; and when his father died in 1461 and he himself was crowned at Reims, it was men from middle-class backgrounds that he appointed as his principal advisers. Caring nothing for their origins or even for their character so long as they were faithful to him, he relied upon them to carry out his policies. But at the first hint of betrayal

he punished them savagely, torturing them and having them incarcerated in those notorious wooden cages covered with iron, some so small that the prisoner could not stand up, which were reserved for the king's enemies in the dungeons of Loches.

Complete tyrant that he was, Louis appeared more like a pilgrim. Dressed usually in gray, with an old felt hat to which was attached the lead figure of a saint, he rode a mule instead of a horse—entering towns by back gates, disdaining all ceremony, eating in taverns rather than palaces. He left it to his wife to preside over his court at Amboise, which he himself rarely visited. Yet this strange, dislikable man did more for the French monarchy than almost any king before him. By bribes, shrewdness, and cunning rather than by force, he brought to an end the declining power of French feudalism and gave his country a unity it had never previously known. He overthrew Charles the Bold, duke of Burgundy, and acquired Anjou and Bar on the death of Count René of Anjou as well as Provence and Maine on the death of Charles II, count of Maine.

When he died at Plessis-les-Tours in 1483—giving instructions for his body to be buried not at St. Denis but on the Loire at Cléry, in a church destroyed by the English and since rebuilt by him in fulfillment of a wartime vow—Louis XI passed on to his son a great inheritance.

This son, Charles VIII, was then a boy of thirteen. He had been born and brought up at Amboise; but although his mother was a studious woman who had kept a large number of books in the château library, Charles never showed the least aptitude for learn-

ing—the only books that interested him were romances of chivalry. Charles, in fact, was appallingly ill-educated. He was also, like his father and grandfather, extremely ugly: small and shortsighted, with a nose like a parrot's beak. His thick, fleshy lips were constantly open though, as he grew older, partially concealed by the wisps of a scattered, reddish beard. His head and hands twitched convulsively; the few words that ever escaped him were muttered rather than spoken; he walked with a crouch and a limp; his feet were so big that he was rumored to have a sixth toe; he was notoriously gluttonous and lecherous. There was something about his restlessness, his wayward, adventurous spirit that, for all his naïveté and assumed affability, made men uneasy in his presence. He dreamed romantic dreams of rivaling the exploits of those great heroes of old whose adventures so impressed him. And he spoke of one day marching into Italy to claim the throne of Naples, on the somewhat dubious grounds that it came to him as inheritor of the rights of the house of Anjou.

When he was twenty-one, Charles made a highly favorable marriage with Anne of Brittany. As if to emphasize its political importance, the wedding took place in the *grande salle* of the castle of Langeais, which his father's chief minister, Jean Bourré, had caused to be built on the Loire to block the path a Breton army might take in an invasion of Touraine. It was a most impressive ceremony. The bride, who had ordered her rich bed brought up the Loire by barge from Nantes, was clothed in embroidered cloth-of-gold overlaid with sable and otter fur

to protect her from the cold air; her attendants were all attired in silk and velvet; her horses were caparisoned in black and crimson. The banquet presented at the royal table included "a sucking pig served whole with a pear between its teeth; a peacock with the tail displayed; several swans, geese and pheasants; then pies which contained live birds which sang most melodiously, and finally a set piece of sugar dishes containing all sorts of figures."

The year after his wedding Charles gave orders for the enlargement and improvement of the château at Amboise, intending—so the Florentine ambassador asserted—to turn it into a palatial city rather than an ordinary palace. And so anxious was Charles to have the building completed as quickly as possible that he employed 170 masons simultaneously, ordering the work to be carried on at night by torchlight and the stones to be unfrozen when the cold winter weather made it difficult for the laborers to cut them.

To overcome the problem of easy access from the town, it was proposed to build two immense towers inside which spiral ramps would allow not only horses but also coaches to reach the terrace. The inside walls of these towers were to be hung with tapestries, sconces, and gleaming candlesticks to make the approach as colorful and dramatic as possible. But the approach, unfortunately, was as dangerous as it was spectacular; and when Emperor Charles V was a guest at Amboise, a careless torchbearer set fire to one of the tapestries. The fire soon spread, and the smoke became so dense that there was some fear the emperor would suffocate.

*In its heyday at the end of the fifteenth century the
castle of Amboise was the most impressive fortress in
the entire Loire valley. Its daunting battlements and
sprawling apartments, recorded by Leonardo da Vinci in
a sketch that has survived, impressed even the worldly
Italian ambassador to the French court. Only a fraction
of the buildings the ambassador so admired are still
standing, however; the outer fortifications were razed
during a 1631 rebellion, and many other structures were
pulled down during the Napoleonic era. The so-called
Charles VIII Wing remains—appropriately enough, for
this luxury-loving monarch was chiefly responsible for
the rapid expansion of Amboise in the 1490s. Charles,
who was born at Amboise, died there in 1498, having
suffered a severe blow to the head in a bizarre domestic
accident. His legacy includes the terrace gardens seen
at right, which were inspired by the ornamental gardens
the king encountered on a state visit to Italy.*

Work on Amboise was well advanced by 1494, the
year Charles VIII rode away to the Alps with an
enormous army on his long-awaited Italian adven-
ture. He entered Naples in triumph; captivated by
the pleasures of the south, he lingered there for
months until compelled to withdraw by an alliance
conjured up against him by Roderigo Borgia, Pope
Alexander VI. The French army withdrew from the
south, every two men accompanied by a mule loaded with loot. Although much of the plunder was lost
at the savage battle of Fornovo, wagon after wagon—piled high with furniture, pictures, sculptures,
fabrics, and treasures of every sort—eventually arrived at Amboise.

Charles had always had a taste for luxury. Amboise now became the palace he had always hoped it
would be—its rooms filled with objects as pleasing
to the eye as they were conducive to comfort; its
floors covered with some two hundred Persian,
Turkish, and Syrian carpets; its courtyard hung with
tapestries and protected from the weather by a blue
awning painted with the sun, moon, and stars.

It was not only the objects of the Renaissance that
Charles brought back from Italy; he also brought
men to propagate its ideas and to practice its arts.
Architects followed him north, as well as sculptors,
scientists and painters, tailors and couturiers, jewel-
ers and scholars, a goldsmith and a confectioner, an
organ builder, a "subtle inventor for the incubation
and hatching of chickens," and the celebrated gar-
dener Fra Pacello da Mercogliano, who was commissioned to design a terrace at Amboise on the lines of
the beautiful gardens Charles had seen in Naples.

Charles had it in mind to do much more both at Amboise and at his other châteaux on the Loire. But two years after his return from Italy, while going with Queen Anne to watch a game of fives in the moat, he struck his head against a low lintel. Although he laughed and made nothing of it, the king lost consciousness during the game and died that same night. He was not yet twenty-eight.

Since Charles's children had died in infancy, he was succeeded by his cousin Louis XII, son of that duke of Orléans who had spent so many years in prison in England after being taken prisoner at Agincourt and who had subsequently sired Louis at the august age of seventy-one. Although only thirty-six, Louis already seemed an old man himself.

Thin, sickly, and rather stupid, the new ruler was expected neither to live long nor to add to the reputation of the French monarchy in what few years might be allowed him. But while he was detested in Italy—where he had served in Charles VIII's army and where he was to lead several armies of his own—he was loved at home for his kindliness and generosity, his simple frugality, and his modesty. So unassuming were his manner and clothes, in fact, that, as the diplomat Philippe de Commines said, he appeared "more like some tradesman or person of low estate than a King." His personal badge, the porcupine, became an object of veneration among the ordinary people of France, who "came several days' journey to see him, strewing his way with flowers and foliage, and trying to touch even his horse with their handkerchiefs, to treasure afterwards as precious relics."

He had been married when a boy to Louis XI's daughter Jeanne, a hunchbacked woman with a crippled hip and a simian face. Anxious to escape from her and to keep Brittany for the crown by marrying his predecessor's widow, he appealed to the pope for a divorce—and in 1498 welcomed the papal legate, Alexander's nephew, the sinisterly charming Cesare Borgia, with a series of splendid fêtes at Chinon. He was delighted to learn that the pope was agreeable to an annulment and that his crippled wife, after undergoing an examination in front of twenty-seven witnesses, could be sent to a convent as useless for breeding.

Louis did not much care for Chinon, which had been virtually abandoned by the court since the time of Charles VII. He spent most of his time on the Loire at the château of Blois, which had been rebuilt by his father and which he himself and his new queen, Anne, decided to enlarge and improve. They built a new wing at right angles to the one erected by Charles of Orléans, then added a chapel behind it. And they brought over Pacello from Amboise to lay out terraces and gardens. Unhappily, Anne did not live long after the new wing was finished. Although of forceful personality, she had never been strong; and in 1514, at the age of thirty-seven, having failed in all her efforts to provide her husband with an heir, she died. Louis was heartbroken. He turned "all the fiddlers, comedians, jugglers and buffoons out of his Court"; and, clothed all in black, he shut himself up in his room where he wept, it was said, for a whole week.

But that same year, driven unwillingly to the

match by political necessity, he married Mary Tudor, the eighteen-year-old sister of King Henry VIII of England. Most men would have been delighted to have such a bride, for Mary was beautiful and good-natured, intelligent and high-spirited. But Louis appeared to be dismayed by the new responsibilities that were thrust upon him. He did his best, however, to produce an heir; indeed, the morning after the wedding he declared that he had "performed marvels." An impertinent spy who had peered secretly upon the marriage bed had a different story: he spread it about the court that it was "impossible for the King and Queen to beget children." In any case, the king was so exhausted by his efforts that three months later he collapsed, never to recover, bequeathing his throne to his cousin, a youth of twenty who succeeded to the throne as Francis I.

The new king's childhood, unlike those of his two immediate predecessors, had been exceptionally happy. His sister, who was three years older than he, adored him; his mother, whose only son he was, spoiled and pampered him. His father, the count of Augoulême, had died of pneumonia when he was a baby, and Francis had thereafter been placed under the care of various governors, the latest of whom was a good-natured Gascon courtier at once kind and companionable. "I think no Prince ever had more pastimes than did my said Lord," a friend of his was later to record; "nor was any Prince better instructed."

Although he had been neither a negligent nor an unresponsive student, although he had attended Mass every day, Francis had always been eager to escape from his books and devotions to the tennis court and the forest. He played racquets as well as tennis; he went hawking and trapping as often as hunting; he practiced at firing the harquebus; he was an expert shot with a crossbow; he fenced; he rode full tilt at the quintain, spearing the target with marvelous dexterity; and he joined his friends in building "towers in which they fought, attacking and defending with strokes of the sword and when they grew somewhat older they began to wear armor and to tilt in every joust and tourney imaginable."

At the age of sixteen he had left Amboise for the somber court of Louis XII, where he shocked the gloomy king with his extravagance and noisy energy. "Ah, we toil in vain," the king had commented sadly. "This great boy will spoil everything." He certainly was a "great boy": far taller than most men of his time, he was also broad-shouldered and immensely strong. His long, fair hair fell to his shoulders, his chestnut-colored eyes were clear and bright; he seemed to glow with health and vitality. Yet Francis was not in the least a handsome youth: his nose was too long and crooked; his mouth was too fleshy and had a sardonic twist; his eyelids drooped heavily. But he was so graceful and charming, so lively and animated that all his faults were overlooked. Even when he romped through the streets at night, disguised and masked, tumbling into bed with common girls and contracting what his mother termed "a disease in his secret parts," his follies were forgiven as harmless, youthful escapades. There was no doubt, it was universally agreed, that he would make his mark in the world.

There were some reservations, however. What
was easily forgiven in a prince was less excusable in
the king of France. When the Venetian envoy saw
Francis stalking into chapel to "attend Mass for the
obsequies of the late king attired in a purple mantle
with a long train," he thought that "he resembled
the Devil." Another Italian, while praising his bearing and generosity, condemned his way of life,
which was "as follows: he rises at eleven o'clock,
hears Mass, dines, spends two or three hours with
his mother, then goes whoring or hunting, and finally wanders here and there throughout the night, so
that one can never have an audience with him."

Wayward as he may have been, no one could deny
the young king's courage. At an entertainment at
Amboise to celebrate the wedding of the duke of
Lorraine, a wild boar charged out of the arena,
where it was being baited for the entertainment of
the guests, and breached the barriers. As the guests
fled in panic, the king calmly advanced toward the
dangerous animal, drew his sword, and plunged the
blade into its neck, killing it with a single stroke. Nor
could anyone deny the king's ambition. Within a few
months of ascending the throne, he marched for the
Alps, reasserting his family's claims in Italy and
declaring himself to be the rightful duke of Milan.
He was determined not merely to see but also to
possess the country of the Renaissance.

In September 1515, Francis won his great victory
at Marignano and returned to the Loire, as Charles
VIII had done, imbued with the ideals that had
inspired the art and learning of Florence and Rome.
In Milan he had seen Leonardo da Vinci's *The Last*

LEONARDO·
·VINCI·

Supper, the superb fresco that adorns a wall of the friary of Santa Maria delle Grazie. Unable to take the masterpiece itself back with him to France, he asked the aged artist to come instead.

Leonardo was reluctant to leave Italy: he was too old, he protested; his work was almost finished; he was not in the best of health. But Francis was insistent, exerting all his charm. He was gracious and flattering: Leonardo knew more than anyone else in the world; he would become "First Painter, Engineer and Architect" to the king of France; he would be granted a generous pension. There was a charming small manor house he could have beneath the battlements of Amboise beside the gentle waters of the Loire. For a long time Leonardo remained unconvinced. According to Giorgio Vasari, it was not until Pope Leo X asked Michelangelo to complete the façade of San Lorenzo in Florence that Leonardo, jealous of the papal favor bestowed upon a rival he "thoroughly disliked," agreed to leave Italy.

Accompanied by his beloved pupil, Francesco Melzi, and his servant, Battista da Villani, Leonardo departed for Amboise. He took with him notebooks, drawings, and several paintings, including *The Virgin, Jesus and St. Anne* and the *Mona Lisa*, both of which are now in the Louvre. He was lodged at Amboise, as Francis had promised, beneath the walls of the château in the delightful small manor house of Clos-Lucé. It was connected to the château by a tunnel, and the king was a frequent visitor to the old man he so revered. Although "struck with a certain paralysis of the right hand," Leonardo continued to draw until his death at Clos-Lucé in 1519,

sketching the outline of the château, which he could see from his bedroom window, designing a canal to link the Loire with the Sâone, and providing ideas for decorations and pageants at the other châteaux along the Loire, châteaux his patron was constantly extending and embellishing.

The first château that Francis had begun to improve and extend was Blois, where work had already started before the invasion of Italy. Here, facing the fifteenth-century Charles of Orléans gallery and the early sixteenth-century St. Calais Chapel—and in striking contrast to the late Gothic red brick wing recently completed by Louis XII—Francis built the imposing Renaissance Façade des Loges, whose stone front, decorated in the Italian style, still looks down upon the roofs of the lower town. The finest achievement of this new wing, the famous octagonal staircase, is not visible on the outward wall; it overlooks the inner courtyard, from which it rises majestically to give access to a series of magnificent rooms on the second floor. There, beneath brilliantly painted ceilings, walls of gilded paneling, and vast fireplaces decorated with Francis' ubiquitous emblem, the salamander, the king held court.

Yet for all the riches lavished upon it, Francis was never content with Blois. Apart from its other defects, it always irked him to remember that it did not belong to him but to his wife, Claude, Anne of Brittany's daughter. Claude had been brought up at Blois; her mother's initial was carved upon its walls; her father had brought Pacello over from Amboise to design the spacious Italian terraces and gardens beneath the Façade des Loges; the fruit of the rare

Blois, like Amboise, is an architectural amalgam, the work of many royal architects over several centuries. The so-called Francis I Wing is not the last or the largest addition to the castle, but it is the finest, marking as it does the triumph of the Italian style.

The wing's most arresting feature is its great spiral staircase, which climbs the outside of the building in an octagonal well, three sides of which are embedded in the façade itself. The stairwell, open between its buttresses (opposite), served as a multilevel balcony.

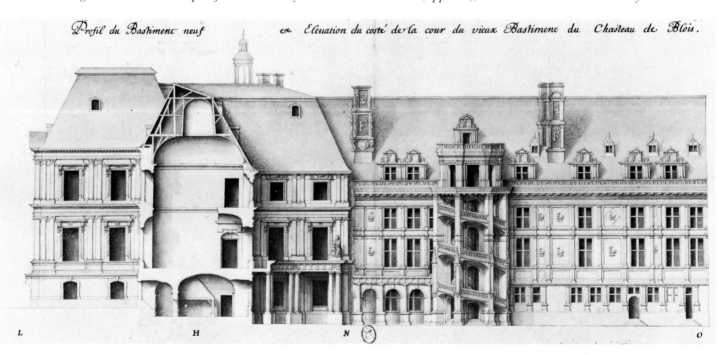

Profil du Bastiment neuf   *Eleuation du costé de la cour du vieux Bastiment du Chasteau de Blois.*

L   H   N   O

Francis I had two great passions, hunting and building, and it was the two, in combination, that led to the construction of the largest and most lavish château in the Loire valley—Chambord. Francis, who interrupted his own honeymoon for a day of hunting, threw himself wholeheartedly into these elaborately choreographed events (near right), which involved packs of dogs, beaters, outriders, and a huge retinue that often included the spunkier women at court. In the forests of Chambord Francis found his heart's desire: deer and boar, hare and wolves in abundance. There was already a small hunting lodge on the site, but it was wholly inadequate to the king's needs, and in 1519 he began work on a new and considerably grander "hunting lodge." To create this splendid new edifice (far right), Francis called upon the talents of the men responsible for the new wing at Blois: Domenico da Cortona, the Italian architect; and Denis Sourdeau, who, with his father, Jacques, had created the grand staircase that graces that wing.

greengage tree, which grew in the gardens and had originally been brought from the Holy Land by Pierre Belon, was known as the Reine Claude.

Francis did not much care for Claude. He had married her immediately after her mother's death, when she had become duchess of Brittany in her own right. As though to demonstrate that a connection with such a plain little thing could be considered nothing more than a *mariage de convenance*, he had gone out hunting the next day. Claude was, indeed, a bride in whom such a man as Francis could scarcely be expected to take much pride. She was "small and strangely fat"; she was lame and she squinted. But she was patient, tolerant, and sweet-natured, putting a brave face upon her possessive mother-in-law's obviously low opinion of her, bearing her husband several children, raising no objection to his continued visits to his several mistresses nor to the gossip that accompanied them. Most of the stories circulating around the court centered on the strong, swarthy, sensuous figure of Françoise de Foix, wife of the sire of Châteaubriant and mistress of the king's best friend, Guillaume Gouffier, admiral of France, as well as of the king himself.

One summer night, so it was related, Francis came to make love to Mme de Châteaubriant when she was already in bed with the admiral. Hearing His Majesty's approach, the admiral leaped from her embrace and hid himself among some boughs that had been placed as a decoration in the open fireplace. Having ravished Mme de Châteaubriant, the king got out of bed and, before leaving the room, paused by the fireplace to relieve himself upon the leaves beneath which the admiral crouched in uncomfortable concealment.

Resignedly accepting such tales about her husband's amours, openly admiring him, and bearing her repeated pregnancies without the least complaint, Claude gradually won his regard if not his love. But he did not relish her company. Having seen to the enlargement and improvement of Blois, where she could supervise the education of their children, he determined to build himself an altogether more magnificent château some miles farther up the Loire. He found the ideal site in the forest of Chambord, where the counts of Blois had built a hunting lodge many years earlier.

The lodge was pulled down in 1519; and work began on the vast new edifice of white stone and blue slate that was to become the biggest and most grandiose of all the châteaux of the Loire. The architect of Chambord is supposed to have been the Italian master Domenico da Cortona, who supplied his patron with a wooden model of the "beautiful and sumptuous edifice" required. François de Pontbriant was appointed superintendent of the buildings; and Pierre Nepveu and Denis Sourdeau were employed as master masons. The central keep, with its circular towers at the four corners, was divided into four blocks by a Greek cross through the middle of which rose an extraordinary spiral staircase, traditionally supposed to have been based on an idea of Leonardo da Vinci's. Two winding flights were superimposed one above the other but never meeting, so that people could ascend and descend at the same time, see each other through apertures

in the central pillar, but never come face-to-face.

This was only one of seventy-five staircases at Chambord; and it was the very enormity of the place, "in the middle of a solitary park," that most impressed Francis' contemporaries. There were eventually to be no fewer than 440 rooms; the park of 13,600 acres was to be enclosed by a wall twenty miles in length, the longest wall in France; the fantastic roof, over 500 feet from end to end, was to be crammed with a medley of turrets and gables, dormer windows, doors, spires, pavilions, lanterns, and as many chimneys as there are days in the year. The magnificent Italianate terrace, flying outward from the keep toward the massive flanking towers and pierced by innumerable windows, provided a grandstand for the ladies of the court to watch the ceremonies that accompanied the return of the hunt. Looking down on the courtyard below, by the light of flaring torches and to the accompaniment of brass horns, the ladies were regaled with the spectacle of hounds being set loose upon the quarry's head before ranks of regimented huntsmen.

Hunting was the *raison d'être* of Chambord. The surrounding forests were alive with game: red deer, boar and wolves, hares and otters. And weeks on end would be devoted to their slaughter in ceremonials as ritualistic as any devised by the Church. Under the grand huntsman of France and the captain of the nets, squads of uniformed huntsmen, harborers, whips, and archers would perform their respective functions in an impressive display that frequently assumed the choreographic nature of a bullfight. An area was enclosed by netting or strips of sailcloth; and when all was ready, the animals would be driven out of the pen in a torrent of wildlife, the waiting sportsmen falling upon their chosen targets with spear or sword as the music sounded. Wild boars would be chased down the rides, brought to bay, and dispatched with elegant thrusts of glittering spears.

Life at court was regulated by the same formal rules that governed the rituals of the hunt. The king himself, after a habitually late night, rose at about ten o'clock and was ceremoniously attired by his attendants. Then, having heard Mass, he dined at eleven. Throughout the lengthy meal he talked to courtiers and scholars, soldiers and priests who gathered around his table, impressing them not so much by the intelligence of his conversation as by his surprisingly retentive memory. Sometimes the meal would be served outside, under the trees by the river (in whose waters the casks and bottles of wine would be placed to cool), the king and his friends talking as they ate the smoked ham, pigs' snouts, sweetmeats, and jellies provided for them by the attendant cooks and confectioners. After the meal, the king would read a book or have someone read to him—romances of chivalry and works on hunting for pleasure; books of history, law, and the ancient classics for more serious moods. The hunt might be followed by tennis, then supper during which jesters did their best to make the king laugh as an aid to his digestion. After supper, he listened to music or watched the performance of a play—or, perhaps, there would be a masque in which an appropriately symbolic part was provided for him.

Much as Francis enjoyed the hunting at Chambord and insistent as he was that work on the château should progress as fast as possible, it was to be many years before it was possible to accommodate there the enormous number of people—almost twenty thousand in all—who followed the court in its constant peregrinations from one Loire château to the next. Once on the move the great company of officials, soldiers, attendants, secretaries, courtiers, ladies, servants, huntsmen, artists, musicians, diplomats, merchants, tradesmen, and hangers-on straggled for miles along the riverside roads. They were followed by hundreds of wagons piled high with furniture and tapestries, weapons and cooking utensils, tents, bedclothes, and provisions. At the same time the river itself would be crowded with boats carrying baggage from one landing stage to the next and with gaily painted barges, including the queen's, with her emblem, the ermine, fluttering on a pennant from the masthead. At mealtimes in the summer, the convoy would come to a halt and moor by the banks, tables would be set up in the meadows, and the passengers would eat and drink in the shade of the trees.

When the destination was reached, most of the court followers were obliged to live in tents or outbuildings or to find lodgings in a nearby town, but the grand master of the household would find room in the château for anyone with just claims upon the king's hospitality. The courtiers could find little cause for complaint. At the king's approach to Blois, for example, his guards would parade on the octagonal staircase in their red, white, and blue striped uniforms, standing ready, tier upon tier, to salute him as he came into the courtyard. Tapestries were hung upon the walls; carpets spread upon the stone walls; his favorite pictures, hunting trophies, and gleaming weapons were displayed where he was accustomed to seeing them; the few pieces of furniture were given a last polish; golden cloths were spread on tables and precious pieces of silver, glass, and majolica arranged around the bowls of flowers; tapers were set to the scented logs in the massive, painted stone fireplaces.

Colorful as was the setting, nothing seemed as radiant as the king himself. "His appearance is entirely regal," wrote an Italian observer, "so much so, that without ever having seen his face or portrait, from merely looking at him you would say at once, 'That is the King.' " He spent a fortune on clothes, having them strewn with precious stones, gold buttons, silver buckles, and embroidered with silks and shimmering metal threads, egrets' feathers, and pearls. A collar of chased gold hung round the neck of his scented shirt; rings sparkled on his fingers. Yet for all the splendor of his appearance, the readiness of his flashing smile, his unfailing energy and apparent confidence, Francis was already in decline.

In 1524 he was only thirty years old, but the triumphs of his glorious youth were never to be repeated. Outmaneuvered and outwitted in his rivalry with Emperor Charles V, his army was defeated at Pavia in 1525 and he himself was taken prisoner and carried off to Spain. When he returned to France the next year, the country was on the verge of bankruptcy and starvation, and the failings of his own

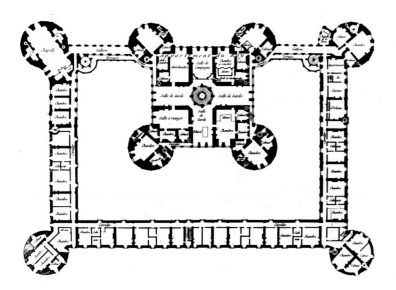

The central keep of Chambord (see floorplan at upper left) is transected by two great hallways, the Salles de Garde. At their intersection is a grand staircase that is this château's most remarkable architectural feature. Its double-helix design (left), with two sets of stairs winding around the central shaft but never meeting, is surmounted by a couronnement, or lantern (above and right), that is seventy feet high.

It is said that Francis I himself did not know the exact number of staircases at Chambord—there are more than a hundred—and gazing at his grandiose château from across the surrounding park it is not difficult to imagine that even a commanding presence like that of Chambord's builder could feel lost within its walls.

character—his inconsistency, selfishness, and shallow flippancy—were by then plain for all to see.

As though resigned to his own inadequacies, and disregarding the poverty of France, Francis continued to lavish money on the adornment of his buildings and the denizens of his court. He still spent huge sums on the dresses of the queen's ladies, on hangings and carpets, on festivals, on the menagerie at Amboise—where he kept bears and leopards as well as bulls and lions to fight one another in the moat—on the extensions at Chambord, and on the patronage of artists.

While Leonardo was still alive, Francis had sent to Italy for Andrea del Sarto, who came to France to paint the *Caritas*. Andrea had since gone home to Italy and declined to return to the French court. Michelangelo also refused Francis' invitation, as did Fra Bartolommeo. But Benvenuto Cellini agreed to come to work in France; he was joined by Francesco Primaticcio, Nicolas Bellini, the Giusti brothers, and Rosso del Rosso, among others.

But neither the pleasures of patronage nor of building brought Francis lasting happiness. Nor, for that matter, did his second wife, Eleanor, sister of Charles V, whom he married after Claude's death in 1524—nor even his new, attractive mistress, the duchess of Etampes. He hunted as eagerly as ever in the forests of Chambord, protesting that when he was too old to ride he would have himself carried after the hounds, that when he was dead he would go hunting in his coffin. He also made love as voraciously as he had always done and continued to stay up late at night. But ever since he had suffered from a painful abscess in 1539, he had shown less and less of his former high spirits.

There were those, indeed, who said that the king had never really been the same man since the death, three years earlier, of his first and favorite son, the handsome, serious-minded dauphin. The christening of this boy, for whom such great hopes had been entertained, had been celebrated with characteristic extravagance and splendor at Amboise. The courtyard had been filled with pavilions; decorations had been designed by Leonardo; a bridge had been specially built from the dauphin's room to the chapel, which was hung with cloth-of-gold and silver; and the bridge itself was lined with Turkish carpets, its roof decorated with countless dolphins. Along this bridge the grand procession had walked toward the chapel, where three cardinals had stood beside the baptismal font. The baby was carried by his godfather, Lorenzo di Piero de Medici, nephew of the pope; the corners of his cloth-of-silver mantle were held by the prince of Orange, the marquis of Mantua, the count of Guise, and the duke of Albany. Now, eighteen years later, the dauphin was dead.

His father was close to death too. Not long after his fifty-second birthday, in the grip of tuberculosis, Francis was informed that Henry VIII of England, three years older than he, had died at Westminster. The news appeared to amuse him: the imperial ambassador saw him laughing with his ladies. He soon grew serious, however; and two months later, on March 31, 1547, he followed his English rival to the grave. Another, more somber chapter in the history of the Loire was about to unfold.

VI

Heirs of "The Shopkeeper's Daughter"

One October day some years before the death of Francis I, his son Henry was married at Marseilles. During the entire ceremony Henry, then fourteen years old, had evinced not the least sign of interest. He seemed, in fact, a listless boy, dull, gloomy, and withdrawn, his lackluster eyes scarcely so much as glancing upon the figure of his bride. She, too, was fourteen, a pale, thin girl "with a rather stout face," her brocade dress blazing with gold, pearls, and precious stones—wedding presents from her uncle, Pope Clement VII (to whom they did not belong, being the rightful property of the Holy See). She was Catherine de Médicis, great-granddaughter of Lorenzo the Magnificent, descendant of those bankers whose great wealth had enabled them to become masters of Florence—yet she was considered by many at the French court to be only a shopkeeper's daughter and thus wholly unworthy as a bride for the royal House of Valois.

These critics of the marriage had further cause for complaint when year after year went by and Catherine showed no indication of ever becoming pregnant. Her father-in-law was kind to her, urging her not to worry, telling her that God would perhaps one day answer their prayers. Catherine did not turn only to God. She consulted doctors, drinking their nauseous potions and submitting to their unpleasant experiments; she went on pilgrimages; she avoided mules because of their infertility; she read books of magic and alchemy and tied charms around her waist. Above all, she sought the advice of the astrologer who had accompanied her from Italy, Cosimo Ruggieri. But she remained stubbornly bar-ren. It was whispered that she had inherited syphilis from her father, who had died of it.

No one viewed Catherine's discomfiture with more contentment than did Diane de Poitiers, the middle-aged widow who, to the astonishment of the court, became Henry's mistress when he was about seventeen. Diane was twenty years older than he, a domineering mother of two grown daughters, but—thanks, so it was believed, to drinking essence of gold and bathing in asses' milk—she was still an attractive woman. Henry remained devoted to her for the rest of his life. Catherine was at first deeply distressed by Henry's evident preference for his mistress; but she soon resigned herself to the inevitable and refused to allow the affair to come between herself and her husband—of whom, for all his faults, she became quite fond as he grew older, less taciturn, and better mannered.

In 1542, an operation having been performed upon Henry, Catherine at last became pregnant and in January of the following year the first of her nine children was born. Delighted at being able to prove to the world that she was fertile after all, Catherine was to find her pleasure overcast by her husband's insistence that Diane de Poitiers should be placed in charge of the children's upbringing. She was also dismayed to learn that, after her father-in-law's death in 1547 and her husband's accession to the throne as Henry II, she was not to be given the Loire château upon which she had set her heart.

This was Chenonceaux, the charming house that Francis I had confiscated from the widow of Thomas Bohier, his collector of taxes, who had failed to pay

over large sums to the treasury. Bohier had bought the estate from the Marques family in 1512 and, because he had to be away from home so much of the time in the pursuit of his duties, he had left the reconstruction of the château to his wife. She had had the whole place pulled down with the exception of the keep and had spent eight years supervising the building—on the site of an old mill nearby—of what was to be one of the loveliest châteaux in the whole of the Loire valley.

Abandoning her claims to Chenonceaux in favor of her rival, Catherine consoled herself by spending hours with Ruggieri—conducting all manner of chemical experiments, studying the stars, casting horoscopes, making astrological calculations, and endeavoring to discover what the future held for herself and her children.

The eldest son, Francis, was betrothed when he was four years old to Mary Stuart, the daughter of James V of Scotland and Mary, the elder sister of the duke of Guise. On his deathbed, King Francis I had warned his son Henry to beware of the powerful Guises, who would strip his "children of their waistcoats," and his "poor subjects of their shirts." But one of Diane de Poitiers' daughters was married to a Guise; and both Diane and Henry welcomed a match that so increased the influence of the Guises in the government of France. So, too, did the little dauphin. He was a shy and sickly child, as difficult and morose as his father had ever been. But he immediately took to the fair, pretty girl from Scotland who had been chosen for him; and as they grew up together, moving from château to château with their attendants and tutors, their pets and playthings, Mary in her turn became fond of him. She would often take him by the hand and lead him into corners where they would trade secrets and kisses.

Their childish happiness did not last long. At a tournament held in 1559 to honor the betrothal of the dauphin's eldest sister to Philip II of Spain, the king rode full tilt into the broken lance of his opponent in the lists. Five long splinters were driven into his eye and forehead and within eight days he was dead. Thus, before he was sixteen, Catherine de Médicis' son became King Francis II.

Catherine herself donned the black dress and the widow's peak that she was never to discard and emerged from the shadows to show that she was now fully capable of ruling her adopted country. She lost no time in dealing with Diane de Poitiers. Ignoring Diane's claims that she owned the château of Chenonceaux in her own right, Catherine demanded its return to the crown. The queen mother did agree, however, to exchange Chenonceaux for the far less attractive Chaumont, the former château of Louis XII's first minister, Cardinal Georges of Amboise, which she had recently purchased and did not like. Diane, it turned out, did not like Chaumont either. She remained there for only a short time before abandoning the Loire altogether to live in retirement at the château of Anet until her death. Catherine moved into Chenonceaux, where she masked the façade with a screen of caryatids, built a gallery on the bridge that spanned the Cher, and prepared plans for the laying out of a new park and two immense courtyards.

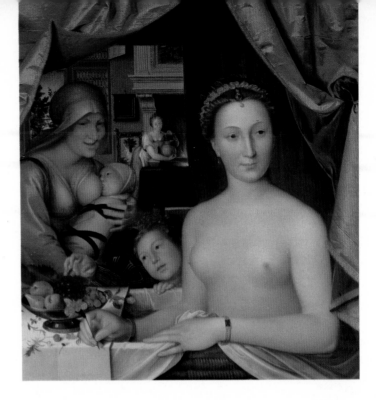

The kingdom was in far too troubled a condition to allow her to spend long in such pleasant pursuits. In defiance of all efforts to stamp them out, the Protestant Huguenots were increasing in numbers and confidence all over France, while enemies of the House of Valois were finding religion a convenient issue in their quarrels with the crown. Indeed, the man whose lance had killed King Henry afterward led Huguenot troops against the crown; and Catherine refused to believe that her husband's death was accidental. She was encouraged in this suspicion by the duke of Guise and his brother Charles, cardinal of Lorraine. Both men were vehemently anti-Huguenot and both were eager to persuade her of the danger in which she and her children were placed by the ambitions of the Protestant relatives of the Bourbon king of Navarre. This king's youngest brother, Louis, the hunchbacked prince of Condé— it was said—hoped one day to become Louis XIII of France by right of his descent from Hugh Capet, the common ancestor of the Bourbons and the Valois.

There was a plot afoot for a large armed band of Huguenots to seize control of Nantes, attack Blois or whatever other château the court was then occupying, kidnap the king, and murder the two Guise brothers. Warned of the plot, the duke of Guise ordered an immediate withdrawal of the court from Blois to Amboise, which occupied a much more easily defended position high above the Loire. By boat and horse the court hastily moved downriver. Orders were given to wall up the château gate and barricade the windows, while squads of well-armed soldiers patrolled the surrounding countryside.

On March 17, 1560, a boatman on the Loire caught sight of a group of about two hundred horsemen trotting down the riverside road toward Amboise in the early morning mist. He rushed back to town to raise the alarm in the château, whereupon Guise hastily called his men to arms, led them out a side gate, attacked the rebel horsemen, and sent them galloping away into the woods. Soon afterward the leader of the rebel forces, Godefroy du Barri, seigneur de la Renaudie, was killed in an ambush. His body was dragged to Amboise and prominently displayed on a gibbet on the bridge with a placard informing all who passed it what his name was and the nature of his crime. While the corpse rotted on display, many of Renaudie's fellow conspirators and Huguenots believed to be in sympathy with them were arrested, tried, and condemned to death. Fifty-seven of them—so it was announced in Paris as well as in churches along the Loire from Nantes to Orléans—would be publicly executed at Amboise.

In preparation for this spectacle, immense stands were erected against the curtain wall of the château. Beneath them in the town square a scaffold and gibbet were built and surrounded by tiered rows of benches for the local inhabitants. Those who could afford it were offered a view from convenient windows. After Mass on the appointed day, the condemned men were led out into the square, proudly disdaining to listen to the monks who had spent much of the previous night preaching in the dungeons and who were still doing their best to persuade the poor heretics to die in the Catholic faith. Many of the victims had reddening bandages about

The kingdom that Catherine de Médicis administered in the name of her sixteen-year-old son, Francis II, was riven by religious factionalism—and less than a year after assuming power Catherine found herself obliged to deal with a Protestant plot aimed at the very heart of the Catholic monarchy: Huguenot conspirators, it was learned, planned to overwhelm the court at Blois and kidnap Catherine and her son. To circumvent this low and dastardly plan, the duke of Guise ordered the court removed to Amboise, a more easily defended château. He then attacked and dispersed the Huguenot forces—and captured fifty-seven of the plotters, who were executed at Amboise in March of 1560. (At right, a contemporary woodcut depicting this grisly scene; at far left, the so-called Traitors' Balcony at Amboise, from which a number of the conspirators were hanged.) It is said that Catherine entertained a large party at dinner in the great hall of the château (near right) on the day of the executions—despite the pervading stench of rotting flesh that filled the chamber and nauseated the guests.

their feet; others could scarcely walk, so cruelly had they been tortured.

Catherine de Médicis, the queen mother, was already sitting in the royal stand; so was the young king; so, too, was his ten-year-old brother, Charles, duke of Orléans. Mary Stuart, however, seems to have been excused as she was subject to fainting fits. The cardinal of Lorraine sat next to the queen mother, while his brother, the duke of Guise, was on horseback in the square below—though the duchess withdrew from the scene, brusquely informing Catherine, "Such scenes revolt me."

The victims began to sing a psalm as the first of their number climbed up the steps onto the scaffold and knelt down at the feet of the executioner. The sword flashed through the air; the head was severed at a single stroke, displayed to the crowd, and then placed on a long bar at the top of a high pole. One after another the heads fell, the bodies being drawn and quartered and thrown down upon an ever-mounting heap by the steps of the scaffold. Men deemed unworthy of beheading were hanged from the balcony of the château (still known as the Conspirators' Balcony) or tied up in sacks and thrown into the Loire from the battlements. The last man to die was Baron de Castlenau, whose cousin, Gaspard de Coligny, was admiral of France and a convert to Protestantism. The spectators shouted for mercy to be shown to Castelnau. But the duke of Guise instructed the swordsman to carry on and the blade fell once more. The court then retired within the walls of the château for dinner. After the meal was over—so the Huguenots subsequently reported—

Catherine de Médicis and her son the king came out again to watch the bodies of the hanged men twisting at the end of the ropes and to see the severed heads falling from the top of the pole.

In fact, although Catherine was as rigid and orthodox a Catholic as the Guises, she seems to have regretted the necessity for the executions and would have preferred a policy of toleration toward the Huguenots—provided they held their services in private. Francis, on the other hand, had none of his mother's subtlety of mind. He was sixteen now, but he was as dim as he had always been, sharing his father's opinion—insofar as he had any opinion in the matter at all—that the only way to deal with the Huguenots was to make the "streets run with their blood." He was quite content, however, to leave all this to the Guises and to devote his time to hunting. Both his doctors and his mother urged him not to tax his delicate body in this way; he would do far better, they said, to take aromatic baths so as to get rid of the poison in his blood that erupted in pimples and blotches on his skin and gave him earaches. (His mother, with this in mind, had a bathhouse specially built for him in the gardens of Blois.) Yet hunt he would and hunt he did until, in the bitterly cold late autumn of that year, when he was taken seriously ill and forced to stay in bed at Orléans.

The young king had been looking forward to several weeks of hunting in the forests of Chenonceaux and Chambord; but on returning from a tiring chase on a particularly cold day outside Orléans, he had complained of a fearful earache, the pain of which had made him faint in chapel. Prompted by the

Like the formidable Renaissance prince for whom he was named, Francis II was a passionate huntsman. He lacked his predecessor's skill, stamina, and good fortune, however, and in 1561, while hunting in the forests of Chenonceaux and Chaumont, the seventeen-year-old king caught a lingering cold. The inept ministrations of the royal physicians only compounded Francis' illness—

and in December he died, leaving his wife, Mary Stuart (with whom he is pictured on the medallion at top right), a widow at nineteen. The hunting museum at Cheverny, a small château due east of Chaumont, is hung with some 2,000 racks of antlers (above), mute testimony to the zeal with which successive French monarchs and their courts pursued the large game of the Loire woodlands.

Guises, who were desperately anxious to minimize the seriousness of their young relative's complaint, the doctors diagnosed a slight cold contracted from exposure to the fogs of the Loire. But rumors flew about that the illness was far more grave than this: a barber had poured poison in his ear; a valet had poisoned his nightcap; the physicians had announced their intention of attempting to cure their patient by immersing him in a bath filled with the blood of young children.

Day by day the king weakened and his agony increased. A lump appeared behind his ear, the inflammation spread upward into the brain, and the doctors, harassed by the Guises, lanced the swelling. By the beginning of December, however, Francis appeared to be a little better. His mother, who had scarcely left his bedside, drove off to Chaumont to consult Ruggieri, who had moved into that château after Diane de Poitiers' retirement to Anet. When Catherine arrived at Chaumont, another astrologer also awaited her there: Michel Nostradamus. In his room in the tower, Ruggieri, helped by Nostradamus, had drawn a magic circle on the floor; on the wall was a mirror with the Jewish names for God written on it in the blood of a pigeon. As Catherine stood in the circle, the mirror misted over, so she afterwards related; it then cleared for a moment to reveal Francis, who disappeared in a flash. Her next son, Charles, then appeared, and after him her third and favorite son, Henry. She waited for the appearance of her youngest son, Hercules; but, instead of him, there came upon the mirror the likeness of Henry, son of the Bourbon king of Navarre.

Warned by Nostradamus that this meant the House of Valois was destined to die out, Catherine returned to Orléans with a fixed determination to marry her daughter Margot to Henry of Navarre as soon as the two were old enough. She was equally determined to obtain the regency for herself if Francis should die.

On December 5 Francis did die, and his ten-year-old brother became King Charles IX. Catherine, as she had planned, became regent. The inheritance was a daunting one: the Estates General was shortly due to meet at Orléans in a huge wooden hall especially constructed for its accommodation; and among the deputies of the Third Estate were several Protestants determined not to be ruled by a woman—a half-Italian woman at that. At the same time there were many other deputies, backed by the Guises, equally determined not to give ground to the Huguenots in any way at all. In her dilemma Catherine turned for help to the admiral of France, Gaspard de Coligny, whom she considered to be a moderating influence. At the same time she ensured that the admiral did not obtain too much influence over Henry by insisting he be taught by Catholic tutors and by moving her bed into her son's room.

Ranged on the one side now were the Guises, determined to support the Catholic faith under any circumstances, even against the crown; and on the other side, the Protestants, who looked to the Bourbon prince of Condé to help them gain their ends, if necessary by force. Thus France became a battleground and the Loire valley once again reverberated to the sounds of war.

In April 1562, the prince of Condé occupied Orléans with two thousand horsemen, intending to make it the Huguenot capital and announcing that he had come to save King Charles IX from the Catholics. Catherine, disdaining help from such a source, asked Condé to meet her at Tours. He agreed at first to come but changed his mind when he learned the size of her escort. Another meeting place was agreed upon, a treeless plain outside Tours where Condé felt more secure from arrest. But when the time for the talks came, he did not feel safe there either. Although it was pouring rain, he refused to take shelter with Catherine in a barn and insisted that they meet out in the open between the serried ranks of their attendants. When at last they did meet, their talk proved fruitless; civil war was judged inevitable.

Fighting broke out soon afterwards. Although Orléans remained in Huguenot hands, one after the other the large towns lower down the Loire—Blois, then Tours, then Angers—were firmly secured by the Catholic royalists. The royalists were also victorious in the open field in Normandy, where the duke of Guise defeated the forces of Admiral de Coligny—who had now come out openly on the Huguenots' side. But as Guise prepared to take his army down to Orléans and thus end the war, a cousin of the Amboise conspirator Renaudie—a fanatically Protestant, "poverty-stricken, yellow-complexioned bony little man" named Jean Poltroy—was sent to assassinate him. As Guise rode back from an inspection of the fortifications of Orléans to the château he was using as his headquarters, Pol-

troy waited for him behind a hedgerow and shot him in the back as he passed. He died six days later, begging Catherine to use the opportunity of his death to bring peace to France.

The next month Catherine and the prince of Condé met in a tent on the Île aux Boefs in the Loire at Orléans and there, at last, they agreed to the terms of a settlement. The agreement, which granted the Huguenots a limited amount of religious toleration, was promulgated soon afterwards at Amboise. But so much bitterness had been engendered that there could be little hope of a permanent peace, and fighting soon broke out again.

Year after year the wars continued—increasingly savage, both sides guilty of the most horrible cruelties—while France grew weaker and weaker, more ruinous and despondent, ravaged by hordes of unemployed workers and bands of vagabonds. The prince of Condé was killed; the young duke of Guise, determined to avenge his father's death, entered the field in the Catholic cause; and Catherine grew old and fat. By the time another peace settlement was signed in 1569, she was over fifty. She was as indefatigable, garrulous, and energetic as ever, but her olive-skinned face was lined and tired, and she was conscious that her sons, for whom she had done so much, were growing beyond her control. "I no longer have the same authority as I did," she told an ambassador. "My sons are men now and I do not have the controlling hand in affairs that I had once."

Charles IX was a disappointment to Catherine. A strong but ungainly young man of limited intelligence, obscenely blasphemous tongue, and ferocious temper, Charles had a passion for hunting that was even more obsessional than his brother's had been. Nor was the chase itself, however vigorous, enough for him; he was never satisfied until he had actually seen blood spurt forth from the cornered animal. When he was angry, he would throw himself screaming to the floor in the manner of the Plantagenets, tearing at his hair and cramming anything at hand into his mouth. He behaved like this on learning that his sister Margot had been caught making love with the young duke of Guise. When he recovered, he had her brought to him, flung her to the floor, and beat her until she was unconscious.

It was now considered essential to have the girl married to Henry of Navarre as soon as possible. The idea revolted her. She was a deeply sensual woman—some considered her a nymphomaniac whose need for men drove her even to lust after her own brothers. But Navarre was one of the few men who did not attract her: he was *dégoûtant*; he never washed; he reeked of tobacco and garlic. She would *never* marry him. But Catherine had decided otherwise. And so on a hot August day in 1572 the wedding took place—the king furiously pushing down his sister's head to make her nod in agreement when her only response to the question as to whether she would accept Henry of Navarre as her husband was to gaze upon the more handsome features of her lover, the duke of Guise.

The duke himself had other matters on his mind. Strolling about in front of the crowds outside the cathedral during the nuptial Mass—flaunting his disapproval of the service being held inside—was the

man responsible for his father's murder, Admiral de Coligny. The duke had never given up hope of having his revenge on Coligny; and he now made up his mind to wait no longer. A few days later an expert marksman in the duke's pay shot and wounded Coligny as he was returning to his house. It was a shot that heralded a massacre.

As groups of angry Huguenots marched threateningly through the streets of Paris, the king was urged to take firm action against them or risk losing the throne. At first he was reluctant to believe he was in such danger; but at length he gave way to the persuasions of his mother and brother Henry, crying out passionately through lips speckled with blood-flecked foam, "Kill the admiral, then, if you wish. But you must also kill all the Huguenots, so that none is left alive to reproach me! Kill them all!"

Catherine had hoped it would be sufficient to kill the leaders only; but once the orders had been given it was impossible to control the carnage. Coligny was stabbed to death and his corpse was thrown out of his bedroom window into the street, where—in the early hours of the morning of that day, August 24, St. Bartholomew's Day—a Catholic mob set upon it, castrated it, and cut off the head. By nightfall some two thousand people had been killed. Protestants and Catholics alike took advantage of the uproar to settle old scores, to plunder, to torture, and to kill. The violence spread from Paris to the Huguenot towns of the Loire; in Angers and Tours, Protestants were attacked and robbed, maimed and killed. At Montsoreau, Jean de Chambes was guilty of the most atrocious murders,

strangling his victims in his towering château and tossing their bodies out into the river. In all, during those dreadful days, as many as seven thousand people are believed to have been killed.

King Charles IX did not long survive the victims of the massacre. As though haunted by visions of the savagery he had unleashed, plagued by horrendous nightmares, he grew ever more gloomy and silent, looking like an old man at twenty-three. He died on Whitsunday, 1574, and was succeeded by his brother, who became Henry III.

Although adored by his mother, Catherine's third son created a far less favorable impression upon his subjects. He was acknowledged to be more intelligent than Charles and better tempered, but he was lazy and ineffectual, content to leave political decisions to others and to devote himself to pleasure. Under his rule court festivities became more and more elaborate and extravagant. There were banquets and masquerades; there were *fêtes champêtres* and carnivals by day, fancy-dress balls and fireworks displays at night. Mock naval battles were staged on the Loire; picnics were held in lavishly decorated gardens or by the riverbank. At Chenonceaux guests would be greeted by ladies of the court, disguised as nymphs or peasant women, appearing from the thickets to offer wine from their "hospitable urns," and by mermaids and sirens singing in the moats. At Amboise there were *bals aux flambeaux* on the terraces, the torchlight flickering on the flamboyant white Gothic walls, pavilions, galleries, gables, and the blue-black pepper-pot turrets. At one memorable and enormously expensive sylvan festival "the

most beautiful and virtuous ladies of the court appeared half-naked, with their hair loose, like brides, to wait upon the guests," while others disguised themselves as men. On such occasions the king himself delighted in appearing dressed as a woman, painted and bejeweled. His subjects, hearing of these escapades, began to call him king of Sodom.

Henry spent most of his time in the company of those beautiful young men who formed his court of *mignons*. Catherine had tried to rid him of his homosexual proclivities: she had arranged for him to be waited on at table by naked women; she had had one of his male lovers murdered; she had allowed him to marry Louise de Vaudémont, a cousin of the duke of Lorraine, a girl whose relatively humble birth rendered her quite unsuitable to be queen of France but who was the only one—so Henry protested—that he could love and be faithful to. Yet, although he remained attached to Louise, he was fond of her as a brother rather than as a husband. They had no children, and he found it impossible to change his tastes. The *mignons* grew in numbers, influence, and provocative behavior, parading through the streets with painted faces and long, curled hair.

Quarrelsome and insolent, Henry's *mignons* were perpetually fighting duels on the pretext of some real or imagined slight; and in one notorious duel a *mignon* whom Henry found particularly attractive was mortally wounded by a retainer of the duke of Guise. Another *mignon*, in a spirit of revenge, seduced the duchess of Guise and was accordingly assassinated by the duke's brother. Henry then swore he would one day have the duke murdered.

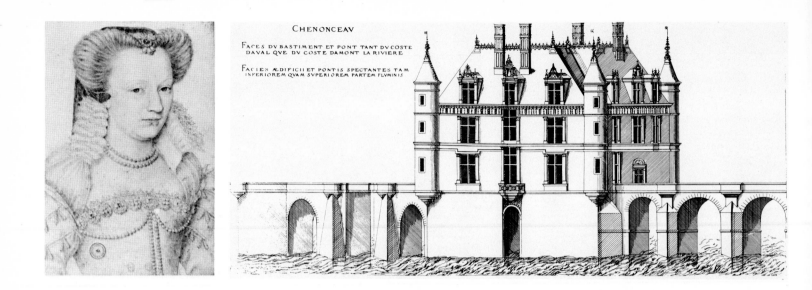

Ten years passed. The effeminate Henry became more and more disliked, the manly duke of Guise more popular. The Catholics turned to Guise as their champion in the continuing quarrel with the Huguenots, whom the king and his mother now thought it better to appease, recognizing that violence served to increase the contagion rather than to cauterize it. The king was driven to forbidding Guise to enter Paris. But he came all the same, was welcomed with the wildest enthusiasm, and it was the king himself who was driven out. He retired to his château of Blois with murder in his heart.

Henry ordered Guise to attend him at Blois. Guise's friends begged him to ignore the summons, but he dismissed all suggestions that the king had any intention of murdering him. "He would not dare," Guise said. "I know him well. He is too much of a coward." Besides, the king's mother, as prudent as she was unscrupulous, would never allow him to risk assassination. Moreover, the Estates General had assembled at Blois, where they met in the immense, painted *grande salle* of the château, and most of the deputies were strong supporters of Guise. He was perfectly safe, he insisted; he never went anywhere without a personal bodyguard that followed him to the very door of the king's bedroom.

When he arrived at Blois, Guise found the king in the friendliest of moods, apparently prepared to give up the government to the new "King of Paris" and to devote the rest of his life to prayer. He confessed that in any case he did not have long left to live: like his brother he was now prematurely old; his hair was falling out, so were many of his teeth; he

no longer experienced the least sexual desire. The queen mother, too, was ill, having contracted a fever at the recent wedding at Blois of her granddaughter to Grand Duke Ferdinando I of Tuscany.

Three days before Christmas, 1588, Guise went to see Catherine in her bedroom, passing through the chamber where, in secret drawers hidden in the paneling, Catherine kept her papers and, so it was said, her bottles of poison. The king was with his mother, and they both greeted the duke warmly. They offered him sweets, asking his advice about the festivities to be held in the château over the coming holiday and talking pleasantly for an hour or so. At last the duke took his leave and went to make love with his mistress, Charlotte de Beaune-Semblançay, a beautiful member of the queen mother's coterie of young girls who kept her informed of all the goings-on at court. The duke left Charlotte's room at about three o'clock in the morning to return to his own—where a few hours later he was awakened with the news that the king wished to see him.

Henry had been up since four, pacing up and down nervously, making sure that various members of his bodyguard of impoverished gentlemen, known as the Forty-Five, were all concealed in the hiding places that had been selected for them. Guise walked across the dark courtyard toward the great octagonal staircase built by Francis I. It was a cold morning, with rain pouring down from a dark and heavy sky. He mounted the steps between double lines of soldiers as the doors were locked behind him, then entered the council chamber. He approached the fireplace and stood with his back to the fire, warming himself, talking to the attendant courtiers, occasionally helping himself to crystallized plums from a scallop-shaped silver box.

Summoned to an adjoining room where he was told the king awaited him, Guise left the council chamber and was walking toward the Cabinet Vieux when a man leapt out at him, grabbed his arm, and stabbed him in the neck. Another of the king's men pushed a dagger into his chest; a third took hold of his legs; a fourth lunged at his loins with a rapier; others entangled a cloak about his sword and drove knives deep into his back. The duke fought back bravely, hitting out at his assailants, breaking the nose of one with his silver comfit box, dragging them all with him right across the chamber and into the king's bedroom. As he stumbled toward the bed, blood pouring down his face, the captain of the Forty-Five laughed at him and tripped him. He fell to the floor; and as he looked up at the king in his dying moments, Henry pushed his face toward the floor with the heel of his shoe. "God, how big he is," Henry said. "He looks even bigger dead than alive!"

On his way to Mass later that morning, Henry called on his mother. "I have had the 'King of Paris' killed," he told her. "I am now King of France."

"God grant that it may be so," the old woman replied from her sickbed, "and that you have not made yourself King of Nothing."

Catherine never recovered from this illness. Nor did the king survive to profit by the murder of the duke—whose body, along with that of his brother the cardinal of Lorraine, Henry ordered burned. The ashes were thrown into the Loire. Early in January 1589, Catherine de Médicis died, speechless at last, in the great bed she had not left since Christmas. And because the people of Paris would not allow her to be buried beside her husband at St. Denis, she was placed in a temporary tomb at Blois. In August of that same year her son, King Henry III, was stabbed to death by a Dominican friar. The more farsighted and adaptable Henry of Navarre, deeming Paris worthy of a Mass, returned to the Catholic faith, entered the capital, and was crowned King Henry IV.

The end of the struggle that had disrupted France for thirty-five years was now in sight; and in April 1598 an edict granting religous liberty to the Huguenots was signed by Henry IV at Nantes. Soon after signing the document, Henry left Nantes for Paris. The Loire was abandoned for the Seine, for the Louvre and Fontainebleau, and for the woodlands near Saint-Germain where Henry's grandson, Louis XIV, was to convert a modest *maison de plaisance* into the palace of Versailles.

The rooms of the forsaken châteaux of the Loire gathered dust, except at Chenonceaux where Henry III's widow, Louise of Lorraine, lived in melancholy retirement for the few years that remained to her. She habitually wore mourning in memory of the husband who had once tried to love her. The mourning was white as royal custom dictated, but all the curtains in the "White Queen's" rooms were black. The furniture, too, was black, the upholstery embroidered with silver tears; heavy black hangings concealed the decorations in the chapel; and on the black ceilings were painted crowns of thorns.

111

VII

Tourists, Revolutionaries, and Invaders

Toward the end of April 1644, the English diarist John Evelyn took the boat that sailed each day from Orléans to Blois, "the passage and river being both very pleasant." Behind the château at Blois, so he recorded, "the present Duke Gaston had begun a fair building through which we walked into a large garden, esteemed for its furniture one of the fairest, especially for simple and exotic plants in which he takes extraordinary delight." This duke was Gaston d'Orléans. Eighteen years earlier, he had been given the château—and sufficient money to rebuild it—by his brother, Louis XIII. The king had made the gift not in a spirit of fraternal affection but in the hope that the duke, who much fancied the idea of succeeding his childless brother on the throne, would find the pleasures of building, gardening, and hunting sufficiently diverting to keep him occupied at Blois instead of meddling in politics at Paris. The duke had begun the work with the utmost enthusiasm, planning an enormously extended château and commissioning François Mansart to design it for him in the newly fashionable classical style. But only a small part of the intended palace had been completed when, in 1638, the queen at last gave birth to a son, the future Louis XIV. There being no further need to placate the conspiratorial duke, funds for the rebuilding of Blois were withdrawn and work gradually came to a halt.

By this time, however, two other fine Loire valley châteaux had been completed. One was the château of Brissac, a huge edifice rising to a height of seven stories. It had been built by Jacques Corbineau for Charles de Cossé, who, as governor of Paris, had opened the gates of the capital to Henry IV. The other was Cheverny, built by Henri Hurault, son of the chancellor of France and a descendant of the builder of the original castle on the site. Hurault's wife, Françoise, had been living in this castle in 1602 while her husband was at court and had alleviated her loneliness by taking her page for a lover. Learning of her unfaithfulness, the king teased the husband about it; and one day, winking to the attendant courtiers, he put up two fingers in the sign of a cuckold behind Hurault's head. Hurault caught sight of the gesture in a looking glass, rode down to Cheverny at a furious gallop, and—still beside himself with rage and humiliation—plunged his sword through the body of the page, who had broken his leg in jumping out of the countess' window. The countess was then poisoned, and it was given out that, being suspected of the murder, the page had been killed for it. Exiled to Cheverny in consequence of the ensuing scandal, Hurault decided to rebuild the château. Work was completed in 1634, and Mlle de Montpensier described the finished product as "an enchanted palace."

Although the château of Sully had been splendidly restored by Maximilian de Béthune—who ordered huge fir trees forty feet long to be floated down the Loire for the new floors of his great rooms—there were, in the early seventeenth century, few other châteaux that would have merited the praise Mlle de Montpensier bestowed upon Cheverny. Chambord, which had been included in Louis XIII's gift to Gaston d'Orléans and which Evelyn had visited on his way to Blois, was certainly not one

of them. Evelyn admired the carvings and the staircase on which the red-bearded and dull-witted new owner liked to play hide-and-seek with his daughter; but he was not otherwise much impressed by the château, "it being no greater than divers gentlemen's houses in England, both for room and circuit." Other travelers lamented its abandoned air, "the gloomy silence of its vacant halls." Amboise, too, was empty for most of the year; the king stayed there only when hunting in the nearby forest and then spent his evenings in the most simple style, even cooking his own food, usually an onion omelette. Chenonceaux had passed into the hands of the duke of Vendôme, but he rarely went there.

Indeed, few of the great châteaux of the Loire were now occupied, and several, like the enormous châteaux of Saint-Romain-le-Puy and Champigny-sur-Veude, had been pulled down altogether. This was in accordance with a decree requiring the destruction of all fortified castles not needed for national security, a decree issued in 1626 by Cardinal Richelieu as a means of curbing the independence of the feudal nobility. Richelieu himself had built an immense château on his ancestral domain south of the Loire in Poitou—unhealthy and unattractive as the location was—and had emblazoned it with gilded shutters and filled it with treasures, "pictures, statues, vases, and all sorts of antiquities, especially the Caesars, in ornamental alabaster." But he seems never to have lived there, the château serving as a monument to his fame rather than as a residence. Nor did Richlieu live at the château of Chinon; after coveting it for several years, he at last managed to

obtain it—though it was afterwards neglected both by him and by his family, in whose hands it remained until the Revolution.

Occasionally Chambord came to life during the earlier years of the reign of Louis XIV, who sometimes came for the hunting and was entertained in the evenings by a play. Molière's *Monsieur de Pourceaugnac* was first performed at Chambord with music by Lully, who also acted in the productions. Playing the part of the apothecary and dismayed by the king's glum reception of the performance, the composer had the bright idea of jumping off the stage onto the harpsichord, which splintered beneath his weight. At this the king cheered up and appeared to enjoy the rest of the play. Molière also produced *Le Bourgeois Gentilhomme* at Chambord; and this, too, the king appeared not to like at first. Nor, indeed, did he look very pleased when it was over. Taking their cue from him, the courtiers—whose behavior Molière had ridiculed in the play—murmured their disapproval. But later the king told Molière that he had enjoyed the play. Predictably, the courtiers changed their minds and decided that they had enjoyed it as well.

The king's visits to Chambord became increasingly infrequent as he grew older; and once his beloved Versailles had become the axis of his life, he felt ill at ease anywhere else. Thereafter the court scarcely ever visited the Loire valley. The stonework of the deserted châteaux began to crumble; the wind blew through the broken windows; and the grass grew long in the parks. The whole of the Loire valley, in fact, was entering a period of decline. Soon the sugar refineries and the stocking and vinegar factories at Orléans closed down; the cotton mills at Saumur, from which so many Protestants fled at the end of the seventeenth century because of the government's religious policies, were also shut; so was the famous Protestant university founded by Philippe de Mornay, seigneur du Plessis-Marly; so, too, were the silk factories at Tours and many of the cloth workshops at Amboise.

Nevertheless, the French spoken in this part of France was considered so pure that numerous foreign visitors came here to learn the language. And the Loire valley, from the middle of the seventeenth century onward, was considered an essential part of the itinerary of that aristocratic institution known as the Grand Tour. Generations of young English gentlemen spent several months at one or another of the towns of the Loire attempting to acquire a satisfactory French accent. Robert Montagu, later third earl of Manchester, for example, spent over a year at Saumur in the middle of the seventeenth century—learning to fence and sing, to dance and play the guitar, and to speak French as well as Latin. He hunted in the forests of the duke de la Trémouille and on the estate of Cardinal Grimaldi. He visited Angers and made the customary pilgrimage to Chinon to see the birthplace of Rabelais—who, it now seems likely, was actually born at La Devinière.

Visitors came to the Loire valley in ever-increasing numbers in the eighteenth century, when the roads from Paris were "incredibly fine," in the words of Joseph Jekyll, a young Englishman sent to improve his French at Blois. "Causeways are as lofty as the Roman ones, nicely paved in the centre, of a vast breadth straight as an arrow for leagues together, and usually planted with trees on either side." The journey from Paris to Amboise could easily be accomplished in the length of a summer's day; and at Amboise there were plenty of boats to take the traveler up to Orléans or down to Nantes. Progress was slow on the river but very comfortable and pleasant. By day there was a charming prospect of wooded banks and white sails, "stately and still as swans"; by night it was "moonlit and serene, and not a ripple of the noiseless Loire interrupted the full concert of the frogs." Nathaniel Wraxall thought that no language could "describe the beauty of the Loire or the fertility of the country through which it flows."

The author Arthur Young, who went to France in 1787, was not as favorably impressed. "For so considerable a river, and for being boasted as the most beautiful in Europe, the Loire exhibits such a breadth of shoals and sands as to be almost subversive of beauty," he wrote. Nevertheless, the towns along its banks commanded his utmost admiration. The entrance to Tours, "by a new street of large houses built of hewn white stone with regular fronts," was "truly magnificent." The center of Nantes was equally "magnificent," all the streets being at right angles and of that same lovely, white local stone; and the Hotel Henry IV, which had sixty beds for masters and twenty-five stalls for horses, had strong claims to be considered "the finest inn in Europe." Nevers presented "a remarkably fine appearance, rising proudly from the Loire"; while the

Lilium persicum Dod.

R. cum pri. re.

Cyanus Vulgaris Lob. Ico.

Ranunculus flore globoso Dod.

Iris Tuberosa Belgarum Lob. Ico.

R. cum pri. re.

Cyanus segetum flore Carneo.

Colchicum pleno flore Clus.

Crocus Satiuus B.

Anemone dicta la Larmoyee.

Lilium purpuro sanguineum flore reflexo.

R. cum pri. re.

beguiling countryside around Orlèans—which contained "near 40,000 people"—was particularly to be admired for "its rich meadows, vineyards, gardens and forests . . . and smaller towns and villages strewed thickly" over a plain through which the Loire "bends its stately way." And if the châteaux appealed to him less than to other visitors to the Loire, he thought Chambord infinitely preferable to Versailles—and a good place for growing turnips.

While Arthur Young was viewing the Loire valley through the eyes of a dedicated agriculturist, the young Arthur Wellesley was at Angers learning how to ride, to fence, and to dance. He was a pupil of M. de Pignerolle, fifth of a dynasty of riding masters whose famous academy lay in the shadow of the château. The future duke of Wellington was "not very attentive to his studies," and he spent a good deal of his time wandering idly about the town, playing with his dog, or dining at the nearby châteaux, particularly at that of the duke of Brissac, who kept open house for M. de Pignerolle's cadets—though he was careful not to waste upon them his best wine nor, indeed, to give them much to eat.

After the death of Louis XIV in 1715, the nobility were more easily able to resist the magnet of Versailles, and new life came to the Loire châteaux. At Chanteloup, the duke de Choiseul spent a fortune on a splendid new palace with a façade that stretched for 350 feet from the chapel at one end of the colonnade to the Pavilion des Bains at the other. At Ménars, Mme de Pompadour's brother turned her château into "one of the first in point of splendour" in the entire kingdom. Montgeoffroy was en-

tirely rebuilt for the maréchal de Contades, whose lovely pieces of furniture can still be seen in the rooms in which they were originally placed. Chenonceaux was restored by the immensely rich Mme Dupin, who employed Jean-Jacques Rousseau as tutor to her sons. "We much enjoyed ourselves in that beautiful place," Rousseau recalled; "and we lived extremely well. I grew as fat as a monk." Montesquieu, Lord Chesterfield, Fontenelle, Voltaire, Lord Bolingbroke, and Mme du Deffand all had reason to pay similar compliment to Mme Dupin's hospitality. The duchess de Choiseul was another charming hostess who presided over her huge household at Chanteloup with the utmost charm and informality, having "no rules for anything" other than the set times for dinner and supper, and allowed her guests to offer pieces of bread to the sheep that wandered into her salon from the lawn. The marquis de Marigny was equally good-natured, rising from the bed to which gout confined him and—in his nightgown—conducting visitors around his château. He once disconcerted Jekyll by pointing out some chairs that had been made in England and commenting in his idiosyncratic English, "How beautiful is your manufacture of horsehair for the bottoms!"

Far more disconcerting, however, was the maréchal de Saxe, who lived in the greatest luxury at Chambord—which had been presented to him in recognition of his service to France in defeating the English at Fontenoy. No longer able to command armies in the field, the maréchal entertained himself by forming a motley array of Tartars, Uhlans, Wallachians, and Negroes into two regiments of cavalry

and training them to perform various tactical movements on wild Ukrainian horses in the park. These horsemen were subject to the most savage discipline, miscreants being hanged from an elm tree reserved for that purpose.

The heartlessness and selfishness of so many members of the French nobility appalled most foreign visitors, who, like Nathaniel Wraxall, were moved with "pity, wonder and indignation" to see "one princely château surrounded by a thousand wretched hamlets; the most studied and enervate luxury among the higher orders of society contrasted with the beggary and nakedness of the people." Jekyll was equally distressed by the miserable condition of the poor and the oppressed: at Blois he had seen "three hundred wretches, chained by the neck like dogs . . . on their way to the galleys at Brest . . . some of them had undergone the torture and could scarce support themselves on crutches."

The abuses of power and the bitter suffering of France's lower classes created a situation ripe for change. When the Revolution came, however, the châteaux of the Loire were constantly threatened but few of them were badly damaged. Abbeys and churches suffered worse: Angers Cathedral was sacked, the statues around the west door defaced, and the interior turned into a Temple of Reason; the abbey at Fontevrault was destroyed; St. Benoît Abbey was forced to close and was then demolished. Numerous church and cathedral treasures, such as the Black Virgin of Le Puy, were smashed. Yet the revolutionary mobs usually contented themselves with ransacking the interiors or gardens of the châ-

teaux—when they troubled to attack them at all. At Chanteloup the paneling was pulled away from the walls, the locks were hacked from the doors, and the lead was stripped from the roof; at Ussé the pictures in the gallery were torn and slashed; at Ménars the garden statues were smashed into fragments. Blois, which had been condemned to demolition in 1788, was spared because it was needed as a barracks, but its statues were removed and the royal insignia cut from the walls. Chenonceaux escaped altogether because even the most fervent Jacobins were not immune to the charm of kind Mme Dupin, whose friend the abbé Lecomte told the local revolutionary committee, "Come now, citizens. Do you not know Chenonceaux is a bridge? Those who talk of destroying it are enemies of public welfare."

Cheverny also survived unharmed because of the popularity of the owners, the Duforts, who declined to flee the country as many of their neighbors had done; the Duforts stubbornly remained in their château despite the attempts of a Jacobin priest to have them ousted by assuring the villagers that they would never be happy so long as they allowed the place to stand with "all those aristocrats inside it." Each morning during the Terror one of the Duforts' servants would walk to Blois for the *Moniteur*, in which the family read of the guillotining of so many of their friends and relations; and every evening they "all huddled together in one small room," Dufort afterward recorded. "And not a single day passed without our hearing of some new calamity." At length the *procureur* of the district, happening to stop at the village inn for a meal, was horrified to

The château of Montreuil-Bellay (left), which stands above the Thouet river south of Saumur, is said to be one of the finest castles in Anjou. It is also one of the best-preserved, having been spared the depredations of the Revolution and its aftermath. The castle kitchen, seen at left in the photograph at right, was directly inspired by the kitchen tower of Fontevrault, fifteen miles to the east. Adjoining the kitchen are four private dwellings, each with its own entrance and turreted staircase. In former times these were used by the canons of the château's chapel—of whom it was said by one chroniclers, "They drank far better than ever they wrote."

learn that the Duforts still lived in the handsome, well-cared-for château across the way. A warrant was immediately issued for M. Dufort's arrest; and, to the indignation of the local populace, their benefactor was inprisoned at Blois. He escaped execution, however, and after the fall of Robespierre was released. He walked away along the banks of the Loire, gratefully breathing the uncontaminated air.

Although many landowners, like Dufort, had reason to feel relieved that the Revolution had caused so little irreparable damage to their properties, there were others who did not escape so lightly when war broke out between the new republican government and the royalist rebels of La Vendée. The Loire valley was the scene of heavy fighting; many buildings were destroyed and large areas of the countryside were devastated. The fine château of Jarzé, near Angers, which had been built at the end of the fifteenth century by Jean Bourré and later bought by a munitions manufacturer from Nantes, was sacked and burned by the Vendéan rebels.

St. Florent-le-Vieil was badly damaged in 1793 when the soldiers of the Vendée, retreating before the republican forces, occupied the town and set fire to the offices of the local government. It was also at St. Florent-le-Vieil that the Vendéan army, again in retreat a few months later, tore houses to pieces in a frantic attempt to make a bridge across the Loire. Doors and window frames, roof beams and floor boards were tied to stakes driven into the sandy bed of the river; and during the night of October 17 and the following morning, tens of thousands of royalist troops clambered across the makeshift structure,

taking with them five thousand republican prisoners whom they intended to kill. The Vendéan commander, the marquis de Bonchamps, had been mortally wounded in the fighting and lay dying on an island in the middle of the river. In his last moments he urged his followers to spare the lives of the prisoners. The order was obeyed; and grateful for the humanity of his political enemy, David d'Angers (whose father had been one of the prisoners spared) carved a moving and dramatic monument to Bonchamps that is now one of the treasures of the Church of St. Florent.

The Revolution over and the Vendée pacified, the Loire valley was left a sorry place. The population of the once-proud city of Tours had been reduced from 80,000 to 20,000. The great châteaux were mostly empty and neglected by their owners, who preferred to live in Paris, leaving "these noble seats," as the English traveler Lord Blayney disdainfully commented, "in the charge of agents or farmers"—or selling them to the rich bourgeoisie. Chanteloup had been bought by "a M. Chaptal," some sort of "*ci-devant* Apothecary," who occupied no more than two or three rooms and eventually disposed of the property to a demolition contractor. No one in Ménars seemed even to know the name of the new owner of the château there—Blayney presumed him to be "some parvenu" living in the capital. The owner of Ussé came to his château just once a year and left it again immediately after he pocketed his rent. Mme de Staël spent more time at Chaumont, but she was always anxious to escape. And when Benjamin Constant asked if she did not at

The most noteworthy architectural feature of Guillaume d'Harcourt's Château Neuf, as the fifteenth-century addition to Montreuil-Bellay castle is known, is the grand staircase—up which, it is reliably reported, the madcap duchess of Longueville once galloped on horseback. Modern visitors to the château come to admire the rooms off this central staircase, particularly the exquisite period furnishings and splendid paneling of the large reception room at right and the faded but nonetheless lovely frescoes of the oratory (above), which date from the 1400's and depict the Crucifixion and Last Supper.

least admire the lovely view, she replied, "I was thinking of Paris, and in truth I confess I prefer the black trickle I see there to these clear and limpid waters of the Loire." Richelieu, like Chanteloup, was demolished for its materials. The buildings at Fontevrault, those that the revolutionaries had not destroyed, were used as a prison. Chinon crumbled into ruins. Napoleon awarded Amboise to Roger Ducos, a former member of the Directory. He pulled down the Gothic buildings of Louis XII as well as the great chapel and sold the materials off to a demolition crew. Chambord was given to Marshal Berthier, who sold the timber and left the building to rot, its ceilings to fall, and its windows to be smashed. Blois was allowed to crumble into such decay that Balzac supposed later generations would know nothing of the château except from his books. Fontevrault, like Saumur, became a prison.

The neglect of man was abetted by the ravages of nature. Three times in the nineteenth century—in 1846, 1856, and 1866—the swollen waters of the Loire burst the dikes, and vast expanses of yellowish water poured across the countryside, drowning animals, destroying crops, submerging buildings. Then, less than four years after the floods of 1866 had subsided, there was a new menace: foreign invasion. War with Germany had broken out, and Bismarck's army had crossed the frontier. Escaping from beleaguered Paris in a balloon, Léon Gambetta, the energetic republican orator, made for Tours. There, as minister of the interior and of war, he carried on the government in the Palais de Justice and quickly raised an army that achieved an early success against the Germans at Coulmiers, north of the Loire near Orléans. It was hoped that, following this success, the army would march north to the relief of Paris. But on October 27, 1870, Marshal Bazaine capitulated at Metz—and the German army continued its westward advance, retaking Orleans and marching down the Loire toward Tours. It was little impeded by the French army's destruction of numerous bridges, including that of Amboise, where the enormous quantity of powder used almost brought down the château as well. Prince Frederick Charles of Prussia established his headquarters in Azay-le-Rideau. When a chandelier crashed onto the table at which the prince was dining, he concluded it was an assassination attempt and threatened to destroy the château as a reprisal.

In Tours, where thousands of refugees had collected and where several Parisian newspapers as well as Gambetta's ministry had established themselves, all was confusion. On December 9, a carrier pigeon brought this alarming message to Paris: "What disasters! Orléans retaken. Prussians five miles from Tours and Bourges. . . . Country laid waste. Brigandage flourishing. . . . Hunger, mourning everywhere. No hope." The next month the German army entered Tours.

During World War I, Tours was again designated as an emergency center for the French government. But it was eventually decided that all the principal ministries ought to move farther south to Bordeaux; and Tours was given the less demanding task of providing accommodation for the administrative staff of the American army.

In World War II, however, neither the town nor the surrounding countryside were able to escape so lightly. Many châteaux were requisitioned for government offices; others were taken over as storehouses for treasures from the Paris museums. The precious manuscripts of the Bibliotèque Nationale were taken to the château of Ussé, which might well have been badly damaged in the subsequent fighting had not an enterprising young woman then living there—the American wife of the duke de Talleyrand—driven over to the German headquarters and persuaded the officer in command to ensure that none of his shells landed anywhere near it.

The French government, led by Paul Reynaud, left Paris for Tours on June 10, 1940. On his way south Reynaud stopped at Briare, on the Loire between Sancerre and Orléans, where Churchill had arranged to meet him. "I displayed the smiling countenance and confident air which are thought suitable when things are very bad," Churchill afterward recorded, "[but] I realized immediately how very far things had fallen."

It soon became clear that the French surrender was inevitable and imminent; and Churchill left for England. He returned to France on June 13, landing at Tours airport, which had been heavily bombed the night before. Since no one appeared to meet him, he and his staff borrowed a car and drove into the city, making for the prefecture, where, so they were told, the French government had its headquarters. The streets were crowded with cars, packed to the roof, being driven away from the advancing Germans. When Churchill arrived at the prefecture, no one of consequence was there. A depressed Reynaud at length appeared to report that the French armies were exhausted and that their lines were pierced in many places. All further discussion was fruitless. Within a few hours the Germans entered Paris; two days later they reached the Loire; the French government moved down to Bordeaux; and on June 17, 1940, Reynaud having resigned, his successor, Marshal Pétain, asked for an armistice.

The German *Blitzkrieg* had caused havoc along the Loire. The center of Tours, including the Rue Nationale, was in ruins; the Pont Wilson and several other bridges spanning the river had been blown up. Orléans and Gien had also suffered heavily. So had Saumur, where officers and cadets of the cavalry school had bravely held up the German advance for three days. At Blois, one of the numerous buildings destroyed was the fine house from whose balcony Cardinal d'Amboise had held conversations with Louis XII in the adjoining château. St. Hubert's Chapel at Amboise had almost suffered a similar fate when a shell exploded on a crossbeam. Further damage was caused later in the war, particularly at Tours, Sully, and Orléans, and at many towns along the mouth of the river: at Donges, which was almost wiped out in an air raid in 1943; at Nantes, where the French Resistance was particularly active; and at St. Nazaire, where the Germans built an enormous submarine base that British commandos attacked in a destructive raid in 1942. By 1945 the French authorities in the Loire valley faced a more formidable task of redevelopment and restoration than had ever confronted them before.

Parts of the exquisite Renaissance château and keep of
Azay-le-Ferron date from the thirteenth century, and
subsequent additions include a tower erected in 1496;
a pavilion in the style of Francis I, master of Blois,
Amboise, and Chambord; and a wing added alongside
the tower during the reign of Louis XIII. But it is not
the exterior, fine as it is, that attracts visitors to
Azay-le-Ferron today; it is the interiors, many of them
furnished in the sumptuous style of the Empire and the
Restoration. Of particular interest are the small salon
at left, with its sunburst marquetry floor and rose marble
fireplace, and the silk-draped Empire bedroom above.

VIII

The Loire Preserved

"This marvelous monument," wrote Balzac of the château of Blois in 1828, "in which so many styles survive, and where such great things were accomplished, is in a state of degradation that is a disgrace to the country." Balzac's was a lonely voice; and it was to be many years yet before any large-scale restoration of the great châteaux of the Loire was attempted. A start was made, however, with the establishment of the Commission of Historical Monuments and the appointment of Félix Duban as architect in charge of the renovation of Blois. But Blois remained for a long time an isolated example of the state's awakening concern for its disintegrating heritage. The château at Angers was acquired for the nation in 1857. Yet it was not officially classed as a historical monument until 1875, and it was still occupied by military engineers until the outbreak of World War II, during which the Germans used it as a munitions depot. The state did not assume responsibility for Azay-le-Rideau until 1905; Chambord was not acquired until 1930. Montsoreau was bought in 1911, but repair work did not start until 1919, and in 1930 several rooms were still occupied by squatters whose predecessors had moved into the largely ruined edifice at the beginning of the previous century. Chaumont did not become state property until 1938. Restoration of the Abbey of St. Benoît-sur-Loire did not begin until the 1940s. Fontevrault Abbey remained a prison until 1963.

Before World War II, in fact, the most important works of restoration were carried out by private owners. When Dr. Carvalho, for instance, bought the château of Villandry in 1906, the buildings had been desecrated by its previous owners and the gardens were a tangle of undergrowth. Patiently and carefully he began the task of reparation, making the château habitable and replanting the grounds so that they once again took on the appearance of those formal sixteenth-century gardens obliterated by the overgrown *jardin anglais*, the natural, landscaped garden so fashionable in the nineteenth century. The reconstructed grounds, based on the drawings of Jacques Androuet Ducereau, master of the bird's-eye view, were laid out on three levels. The kitchen garden, where vegetables grow in neat, geometrical patterns between straight gravel paths, is on the lowest level. Above this is the ornamental *jardin d'amour*, a complicated composition of heart-shaped, square-cut box borders and trimly clipped yew trees. Above the *jardin d'amour* is the water garden, whose expanse of smooth water is circumscribed by rows of lime trees. These unique gardens have been meticulously maintained by Dr. Carvalho's son, who planted an apple orchard to complement his father's work.

The château of Chenonceaux was also restored by a wealthy private owner, who returned it to its original appearance. Mme Pelouze walled up the windows with which Catherine de Médicis had defaced the sixteenth-century façade, banished the ungainly caryatids to the park, and pulled down the decorated entrance masking the east front. Mme Pelouze's dedicated restoration efforts have been continued by the Menier family, the chocolate manufacturers who own the château today.

Soon after the restoration of Chenonceaux was undertaken, work began on Chaumont. It had been bought by Prince Amédée de Broglie and his rich wife, Marie, who spent their honeymoon there in 1875 and subsequently determined not merely to rebuild the château but even to remove the two villages, Place and Fradillet, that had grown up in the park beneath its walls. One by one the houses in these villages were purchased and their residents provided with accommodations in a new village closer to the river. The empty buildings were then demolished and carted away, while the old church was taken down and rebuilt in a less conspicuous position—so that the prince and princess could enjoy the pleasures of an English park without any impediment to their view from the windows of the château. All this cost a great deal of money, and the Broglies, rich as they were, became obliged to consider means of making economies in expenditure. It was suggested that the family elephant—a present from an Indian maharajah, which was kept in the stables and munched its way through an enormous quantity of food each day—might be relegated to a zoo. But this measure was rejected as unnecessarily extreme; and it was decided instead that the family should for the time being make the rather less demanding sacrifice of giving up their customary *paté de foie gras* sandwiches with afternoon tea.

Princess de Broglie's sister Jeanne married the son of the duke of Brissac, whose family had moved out of their château after the Revolution and built a smaller house in the park. Jeanne's fortune enabled them to restore the old château, which is still occupied by the Brissac family. Another great fortune, that of the Siegfrieds, made possible the restoration and furnishing of the château of Langeais. At Cheverny, descendants of the Huraults, the Vibrayes, bought the château back for the family in 1825; they continue to maintain it in excellent order today.

All these châteaux are now open to the public; and at many of them performances are given of that new form of entertainment known as *son et lumière*, which was first presented at Chambord in 1952. Although most of the châteaux of the Loire have now been extensively and sympathetically restored, it has not been possible to make the river itself navigable again. It has always been an unpredictable river, its rate of flow varying from a placid trickle in the summer to a raging torrent after the melting of the winter snow, when a rush of almost 300,000 cubic feet a second has been measured at Orléans. Yet until the late nineteenth century it was one of the busiest waterways in France.

In the time of the Bourbon kings travelers saw numerous flat-bottomed barges with big square sails sailing up and down the Loire with all manner of cargoes: timber and coal, grain and oil, casks of wine from the vineyards of Anjou and Touraine, cases of pottery from Nevers, looms and ropes from Angers, vinegar and preserved vegetables from Orléans, boxes of religious medallions from Saumur, and bales of silk from Tours. "There are many barges and boats at the quay," wrote Arthur Young of Orléans in the eighteenth century. "They are loaded with wood, brandy, wine and other goods. On arriving at Nantes the vessels are broken up and sold

The moated château of Villandry, which stands on a rise above the confluence of the Loire and the Cher, is an interesting structure in its own right. Built in the sixteenth century by Jean le Breton, who was secretary of state under Francis I, the three residential wings of the château enclose a central court of honor—and frame a splendid vista of the Loire valley. Since the 1930s, however, the principal attraction of Villandry has been its gardens, restored to their former glory through the largesse of the Carvalho family. Other Loire châteaux have extensive plantings, but only Villandry has gardens laid out in the sixteenth-century French manner (right). These showcase plantings are terraced, with a kitchen garden on the lowest level and a severely geometric ornamental garden of carefully clipped yew and box tree hedges above that. The topmost tier is a jardin d'eau— 8,400 square yards of water jets, cascades, canals and fountains interspersed with pergolas and statuary.

with the cargo." The journey, Young added, took about four and a half days. In actual fact it usually took much longer, and shippers at Nantes had been known to wait as long as six months for cargoes to reach them from Orléans. With the advent of the steamboat in the 1830s, the journey time was cut to two days; and four companies were formed to meet the demands of both passengers and merchants for this new, quick method of transportation. The rivalry between the companies was intense; in competition with one another to reduce the time of the journey still further, captains allowed their boilers to build up such a pressure that they often burst.

An enterprising company launched the *Inexplosibles*, long paddle steamers with tall funnels, whose boilers were guaranteed against explosion. These *Inexplosibles* were less liable, so their advocates maintained, to become grounded on the sandbanks and less inclined to cover passengers with the soot that fell from the clouds of black smoke produced by the soft coal used by their rivals. They were certainly popular. In 1843 more than 100,000 passengers paid to take a journey on the Loire either in one of these paddle steamers or in the faster and more comfortable *Etincelle* ("The Spark"), the largest boat ever to sail on the Loire. But the short life of the Loire steamboats was already nearing its close.

In the early 1840s the railway line from Paris to Orléans was opened; and this was soon followed by an extension to Tours, then to Nantes, then by a network of lines that robbed the Loire of nearly all its traffic, despite the fierce price-cutting of the steamboat companies. The traffic never returned to

The Loire is a fickle river: a rampaging torrent when autumn rains fall, it dries to a silt-choked trickle by later summer—a "river" of golden sand. Never an easy river to navigate because of its strong currents and numerous sand bars, the Loire nonetheless served as the valley's principal commercial artery from Roman times until the middle of the nineteenth century, when the coming of the railroad put an end to the steamboat traffic (left) that regularly carried as many as 100,000 passengers a year along the waterway. Fate, equally fickle, has brought periods of great prosperity and even greater devastation to the region known as "the garden of France." In 1940, for instance, the bridge across the Loire at Amboise (right) was damaged by bombing— but it was precisely this sort of damage that led to the extensive restoration of many Loire valley châteaux in the decades immediately following World War II.

the river. An occasional boat can be seen nowadays in the upper reaches; a few fishing boats still sail langorously about in the neighborhood of Nantes; barges chug down the estuary; quite large ships can sail as far as Donges from St. Nazaire. But of that great river activity that tourists described two hundred years ago nothing is left. Huge quantities of silt, brought down into the Loire from its numerous tributaries, have clogged the riverbed and formed islands of sandy sediment that block the passage of boats of even the shallowest draught.

The Loire remains, however, a fisherman's paradise. There are quantities of crayfish and mountain trout in the river and its numerous small tributaries; perch, carp, and pike as well as trout can be caught around Bas-en-Basset, south of Le Puy-en-Velay; shad and salmon are still occasionally to be found near Chinon; the backwaters abound with eel. Pollution, of course, has taken its toll. When the waters were clearer, bleak and bream, roach, gudgeon, barbel, and chub were all plentiful. Now the last of them have gone, although efforts are being made to bring them back.

In the meantime, the fish of the Loire continue to appear in gratifying abundance on the tables of the valley's restaurants—an ancillary pleasure of any visit to the châteaux country. These include mullet and pike with white butter sauce, stuffed bream and stuffed carp, baked tench, sorrel-flavored chad, and eels simmered in old wine. Indeed, the Loire valley is renowned for its cuisine, which exerts the same pull on the gourmet that the châteaux do on architecture buffs and amateur historians. For some the region's splendid cooking is an added attraction; for others, it is *the* attraction—with visits to the restored châteaux serving to break up the gourmandizing. Nantes is justly celebrated for its *caneton au muscadet* as well as for its eel roe and stuffed cockles; Angers, like Tours, for its potted pork, chitterlings, and *boudins blancs*; Orléans and Blois for veal pasty, quail pie, and jugged hare; Tours for *gogues* and *meringues à la crème fouettée*; Chinon for *saumon de la Loire;* Amboise for *foie confit au Vouvray*; Sancerre for goats' milk cheese. The pears and apricots of Angers, the plums of Tours, and the strawberries of Saumur are nonpareil.

The local wines are also world-famous. There is a legend that the art of pruning vines was taught to the fourth-century monks of the Abbey of Marmoutier by their donkeys. Having wandered out of the field where they were kept, the animals nibbled the leaves and shoots of the vines down to the stocks. The monks, thinking the vines had been ruined, were astonished to discover that they bore far better grapes the following year than the vines the donkeys had left untouched. Ever afterward the monks of Marmoutier pruned their vines; and the wines of the district—the excellent, slightly sweet wines of Vouvray, both still and *petillant*—have always been among the most prized in France. Comparable to these, but slightly drier, are the white wines of the Saumur region and the richer, fruitier wines of the Coteaux du Layon. Among the drier white wines are the delicious Pouilly-Fumé, made from the Sauvignon grape, which grows in the vineyards on the east side of the river between Cosne and La Charité, and the

rather coarser Pouilly-sur-Loire, which comes from the same area but is made from the Chasselas grape. Also from this area, though on the other side of the river, are the dry white wines of Quincy, Reuilly, and the superb Sancerre, which is surely the finest moderately priced white wine that France has to offer.

Most of the Loire's best wines are white. But from the department of Indre-et-Loire come those two splendid red wines, Chinon and Bourgueil, both of which are an ideal complement to two local delicacies, *coq au vin du pays* and *gibier de Sologne*. You will also find in this region some good Coteaux de Touraine rosé, wines that are less sweet than the better known rosé d'Anjou.

The white, chalky hillsides of the Loire provide ideal cellars for its wines and for the meetings of the viticulturists' fraternities, such as the Chantepleure of Vouvray and the Sacavins of Angers. They also provide ideal places for a *dégustation de vin* among the rows of barrels of *vin ordinaire* and the thousands of bottles whose colored tops can be seen jutting out from the holes in the rock. But the best place to drink wine is at a table with the prospect of good food before you, and two of the best restaurants in France are on the Loire: the Frères Troisgros at Roanne and the Barrier at Tours. There are also extremely good restaurants at Langeais, Moulins, Montrond-les-Bains, and Feurs. Moreover, the Loire valley is exceptionally well provided with those comparatively cheap restaurants where ill-cooked food is almost never encountered.

The local people you will see in these restaurants and those who will serve you there are as pleasant,

good-natured, and easy-going as you could hope to find anywhere. There is a story told in Touraine that when the remains of St. Martin were being brought to Tours, cripples and invalids hurried to touch them and were instantaneously cured. Two crippled beggars were urged to join the throng; but, rather than lose their livelihood, they hurried away as fast as their wasted legs and crutches would carry them. They were not quick enough, however: the procession caught up with them, and the very proximity of the holy relics brought about the unwanted cure. Complacently accepting that they could no longer live on charity as beggars, they decided to continue to avoid manual labor by going into the preaching business. At this they were so successful that they raised enough money to build a chapel and a village at Chapelle-sur-Loire, where they settled down in contented retirement. In this legend, the amiable, indolent, yet imaginative and resourceful nature of the men of the Loire valley is exactly portrayed. "All good Tourangeaux are as simple as their lives," wrote Alfred de Vigny, who was born at Loches, "as gentle as the air they breathe, as strong as the rich soil they till. Their brown features show neither the coldness of the north nor the vivacity of the south."

The people of Anjou are said to be less open than the Tourangeaux, more canny, even calculating. Those who live in the mountainous regions are sometimes said to have acquired a character in tune with their rugged winter landscape. But, in fact, the differences are imaginary rather than real: the people of the Loire are all much alike. Only the Bretons of the Loire estuary have a distinctive character of

their own; and they, after all, are a different race, ethnically and linguistically closer to the Welsh than they are to the French.

The diversity of the Loire valley is in the landscapes rather than the people—the wild, rugged uplands of the Vivarais Mountains where sheep graze amid the flowers and shrubs in the shadows of huge outcrops of volcanic rock; the tree-covered slopes of the gorges where ruined châteaux stand guard above the rushing water and kingfishers can still be seen along the remoter reaches; the fertile meadows of the Forez plain, where the corn is rich and the waterfowl abundant in the thick, green reeds; the wide pastures of the plain of Roanne with their herds of white cows by the river's bank; the green hills of the Nivernais, on whose gentle slopes Charollais cattle gaze dreamily at the grass. Beyond Nevers the vineyards begin, and then the valley opens out and the river turns now this way now that as it winds its way to Orléans past lines of poplars and willow trees, market gardens as well as vineyards, fields of vegetables, young ornamental trees, and rose bushes.

From the Orleanais the Loire enters Touraine; and already the mild climate, blue skies, and gentle breezes offer a welcome to what a fifteenth-century Florentine was first to call the "Garden of France." Soon the vines and corn, the fruit and vegetables are joined by vegetation of a Mediterranean character, by camellias and hydrangeas growing wild, fig trees, palm, and eucalyptus. As Tours comes into sight the limestone and tufa of the riverside give way to hills of flintstone, which provide the local wines with their distinctive flavor. Then, downstream from Blois, tufa is once again found below the vineyards; and it is in this soft white stone that the Tourangeaux, since time immemorial, have been digging cave dwellings and living as troglodytes, so that it is possible even today to see the smoke of some kitchen fire rising up into the blue sky from the middle of a field and to consider the possibility of an unwary rabbit falling headlong into the housewife's cooking pot. The river flows through Touraine, then into Anjou, where the "meadows are ever clad in green and the vines adorned with grapes," and at last into Brittany and out to sea.

This picture of the Loire valley as a peaceful, idyllic countryside, untroubled by the commerce of modern man, is not a fanciful one. There are industries in the valley, of course. St. Etienne and Orléans are both large industrial centers; Nantes is still growing and St. Nazaire is now one of the busiest of French ports; there are glassworks in the Forez and slate quarries near Angers; the forges of the Nivernais, famous for centuries and responsible for parts of the Eiffel Tower, are still in operation; so are the potteries of Nevers; nuclear power stations have altered the landscape near Chinon, as the oil refineries have at Donges and as the discovery of uranium is likely to do near Roanne.

But the Loire valley remains essentially a quiet, gentle region of green meadows, sloping farmlands, vineyards, orchards, gardens—and châteaux. A region, moreover, that occasionally seems deliberately to have turned its back on the modern world and chosen to live in the past.

THE LOIRE IN LITERATURE

Arthur Young, longtime editor of an eighteenth-century journal called Annals of Agriculture, *was by profession a specialist in agricultural economy—and by preference a peripatetic journalist. Young's* Tour in Ireland, *published in 1780, was followed, twelve years later, by* Travels in France during the years 1787, 1788 and 1789, *from which the ensuing description of the central Loire valley and its châteaux is taken.*

The 5th. Through a dead flat and unpleasant country, but on the finest road I have seen in France—nor does it seem possible that any should be finer; not arising from great exertions, as in Languedoc, but from being laid flat with admirable materials. Chateaus are scattered every where in this part of Touraine; but farm houses and cottages thin, till you come in sight of the Loire, the banks of which seem one continued village. The vale, through which that river flows, may be three miles over; a dead level of burnt russet meadow.

The entrance of Tours is truly magnificent, by a new street of large houses, built of hewn white stone, with regular fronts. This fine street, which is wide, and with foot pavements on each side, is cut in a strait line through the whole city to the new bridge, of fifteen flat arches, each of seventy-five feet span. It is altogether a noble exertion for the decoration of a provincial town. Some houses remain yet to be built, the fronts of which are done; some reverend fathers are satisfied with their old habitations, and do not choose the expence of filling up the elegant design of the Tours projectors; they ought, however, to be unroosted if they will not comply, for fronts without houses behind them have a ridiculous appearance. From the tower of the cathedral there is an extensive view of the adjacent country; but the Loire, for so considerable a river, and for being boasted as the most beautiful in Europe, exhibits such a breadth of shoals and sands as to be almost subversive of beauty.

The 11th. To Blois, an old town, prettily situated on the Loire, with a good stone bridge of eleven arches. We viewed the castle, for the historical monument it affords that has rendered it so famous. They shew the room where the council assembled, and the chimney in it before which the Duke of Guise was standing when the king's page came to demand his presence in the royal closet: the door he was entering when stabbed: the tapestry he was in the act of turning aside: the tower where his brother the cardinal suffered; with a hole in the floor into the dungeon of Louis XI of which the guide tells many horrible stories, in the same tone, from having told them so often, in which the fellow in Westminster Abbey gives his monotonous history of the tombs. The best circumstance attending the view of the spots, or the walls within which great, daring, or important actions have been performed, is the impression they make on the mind, or rather on the heart of the spectator, for it is an emotion of feeling, rather than an effort of reflection. The murders, or political executions perpetrated in this castle, though not uninteresting, were inflicted on, and caused by men who command neither our love, nor our veneration. The character of the period, and of the men that figured in it, were alike disgusting. Bigotry and ambition, equally dark, insidious, and bloody, allow no feelings of regret. Quit the Loire, and pass to Chambord. The quantity of vines is great; they have them very flourishing on a flat poor blowing sand. How well satisfied would my friend Le Blanc be if his poorest sands at Cavenham gave him 100 dozen of good wine per acre per annum! See at one *coupe d'oeil* 2000 acres of them. View the royal chateau of Chambord, built by that magnificent prince Francis I and inhabited by the late Marechal de Saxe. I had heard much of this castle, and it more than answered my expectation. It gives a great idea of the splendour of that prince. Comparing the centuries, and the revenues of Louis XIV and Francis I I prefer Chambord infinitely to Versailles. The apartments are large, numerous, and well contrived. I admired the stone stair-case in the centre of the house, which, being in a double spiral line, contains two distinct stair-cases, one above another, by which means people are going up and down at the same time, without seeing each other.

The 15th. Cross, for a considerable distance, the royal oak forest of Sénart. About Montgeron, all open fields, which produce corn and partridges to eat it, for the number is enormous. There is on an average a covey of birds on every two acres, besides favourite spots, where they abound much more. At St. George the Seine is a much more beautiful river than the Loire. Enter Paris once more, with the same observation I made before, that there is not one-tenth of the motion on the roads around it that there is around London. To the hotel de la Rochefoucauld.—20 miles.

The 16th. Accompanied the Count de la Rochefoucauld to Liancourt.—38 miles.

I went thither on a visit for three or four days; but the whole family contributed so generally to render the place in every respect agreeable, that I staid more than three weeks. At about half a mile from the chateau is a range of hills that was chiefly a neglected waste: the Duke of Liancourt has lately converted this into a plantation, with winding walks, benches, and covered seats, in the English style of gardening. The situation is very fortunate. These ornamented paths follow the edge of the declivity to the extent of three or four miles. The views they command are every where pleasing, and in some places great. Nearer to the chateau the Duchess of Liancourt has built a menagerie and dairy in a pleasing taste. . . .

ARTHUR YOUNG
Travels in France, 1792

Left: Catherine de Médicis' oratory at Blois; below: the great hall, used for meetings of the Estates General; lower right: diagram of the château and its extensive gardens.

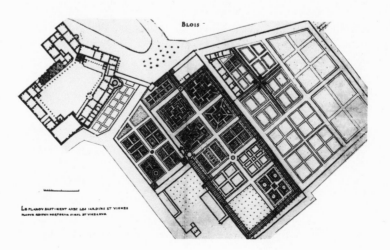

She was the familiar of virtually every important belle-lettrist of the post-Revolutionary period, and she was an acknowledged influence on such later writers as Lamartine and Victor Hugo. She is regarded by some as the creator of the modern "feminist" novel—and, 175 years after her death, she is still read and discussed. She was born Anne Louise Germaine Necker, daughter of Jacques Necker, the French minister of finance, but she is known universally by her married name, Mme de Staël. An unbridled and acid-tongued critic of Napoleon, Mme de Staël was banished from Paris several times during the turbulent early decades of the nineteenth century. Ten Years of Exile, *her chronicle of that period, includes this description of a stay in the Loire valley.*

Since the owner of the Château of Chaumont had returned from America, I was no longer able to stay there, so I settled on the estate called Fossé, which a generous friend lent me. The estate was the home of a Vendéen soldier who was somewhat careless of its upkeep, but his good nature and ready wit made me feel at ease. We hardly had arrived when the Italian musician who was with us to give lessons to my daughter began to play the guitar, and my daughter, her harp, to accompany the sweet voice of my beautiful friend Madame Récamier, while peasants gathered at the windows, astonished to see this group of troubadours who had come to enliven their master's solitude. I spent my last days in France there, with a few friends of whom I still have fond memories.

Certainly this intimate group in this solitary residence, and our agreeable preoccupation with the fine arts did no harm to anyone. We often sang a charming tune composed by the Queen of Holland with the refrain "Do what you ought, come what may." After dinner, we thought up the idea of seating ourselves around a green table and writing notes

to each other instead of conversing. These many and varied tête-à-têtes amused us so much that we were impatient to leave the dinner table—where we spoke to each other normally—to go and write to each other. When chance strangers arrived, we could not bear to interrupt our diversion and our "little post office" (which is what we called it) kept on going all the same. The inhabitants of the neighboring town were somewhat astonished at our ways, and considered them pedantry, whereas this game was only an expedient against the monotony of solitude. One day a gentleman of the vicinity who had never thought of anything but hunting all his life came to take my sons on an outing to his woods. He remained seated for a while at our active, silent table; in her pretty handwriting, Madame Récamier composed a little note to this rough hunter, so that he would not feel too much of a stranger in our circle. He declined with apologies, assuring us that he could not read the writing in the lamplight. We laughed a little at this blow to our beautiful friend's benevolent coquetry and we thought that a note from her hand would not always have had the same fate. Our days were spent in this way, and if I may judge from my own experience, no one felt the time to be a burden. . . .

My two sons tried to see the Emperor at Fontainebleau, where he was at that time; they were told they would be arrested if they remained there; all the more reason why I myself was prohibited from going. I had to return to Switzerland from Blois, where I was staying, without going nearer to Paris than forty leagues. The Minister of Police had said—in privateering jargon—that at thirty-eight leagues "I was a lawful prize"; that was his piratical-minister expression. Thus, when the Emperor exercises the arbitrary right of banishment, neither the exiled person, nor his

Three interiors at Chaumont, left to right: the dining room, reception hall, and Catherine de Médicis' bedroom.

141

friends, nor even his children, can reach him to plead the cause of the unfortunate who is being torn from the objects of his affections and his habits; and these banishments, which now are irrevocable—especially in the case of women—these banishments, which the Emperor has rightly termed "proscriptions," are decreed without the victim's being allowed to present any defense, assuming that the crime of having displeased the Emperor even allows for any.

Although I had been restricted to forty leagues, I had to pass through Orléans, a rather dull city but the residence of some very pious women who have taken refuge there. While strolling through the town I stopped in front of the monument to Joan of Arc. "Certainly," I thought, "when she delivered France from the English, even then, France was freer by far, and more truly France than she is at the present time." Wandering through a town where you are neither known nor recognized by anyone is an odd sensation. I felt a kind of bitter pleasure in contemplating my own isolation, and in looking once more at the France I was about to leave—perhaps forever—without speaking to anyone, without anything to distract me from observing the country itself. Passers-by occasionally stopped to look at me, because I think that in spite of myself I had a woeful expression; but they quickly went on their way, for people have long since grown accustomed to seeing suffering.

MADAME DE STAËL
Ten Years of Exile, 1821

A TALE OF THREE CHÂTEAUX

Alexandre Dumas is best known today for such rollicking historical romances as The Count of Monte Cristo *and* The Three Musketeers, *but during Dumas* père's *own lifetime his so-called Valois romances numbered among the more popular titles by this most prolific of writers, whose output included three hundred novels.* The Lady of Monsoreau— *Monsoreau being the name of a famous Loire valley château—is the second volume of Dumas' Valois trilogy, and it deals with an achial historical incident: the attempted seduction of Diane de Méridor by the duke of Anjou. It contains all the elements of swashbuckling romance, including cryptic notes, mysterious locked doors, a precipitate flight to the château of Lude in disguise, and abduction by brigands. This particular passage begins with Diane's resistance to the suit being brought by the baron of Monsoreau—the lesser of two evils, as it turns out—and ends with her imminent release from the clutches of the conniving duke of Anjou.*

One morning my father entered my chamber, looking graver than usual, but there was an air of satisfaction blended with his gravity.

"My child," said he, "you have always assured me that you would never like to leave me!"

"Ah! father, are you not aware that it is my fondest desire to be with you forever?"

"Well, my own Diane," he continued, stooping to kiss me, "it depends entirely on yourself whether that desire shall be realized or not."

"I suspected what he was about to say, and I turned so frightfully pale that he paused before touching my forehead with his lips.

"Diane, my child! Good heavens! what is the matter?"

"It is M. de Monsoreau, is it not?" I stammered.

"And supposing it is?" he asked, in amazement.

"Oh, never, father! if you have any pity for your daughter, never!"

"Diane, my darling, it is not pity I have for you, it is idolatry, as you well know; take a week to reflect and, if in a week"—

"Oh, no, no," I cried, "it is needless,—not a week, not twenty-four hours, not a minute. No, no; oh, no!"

And I burst into tears.

My father worshipped me; he had never seen me weep before; he took me in his arms, and, with a few words, set me at my ease; he pledged his word of honor he would never again speak of this marriage.

And now a month slipped by, during which I neither saw nor heard anything of M. de Monsoreau. One morning my father and I received an invitation to a great festival the count was to give in honor of the King's brother, who was about to visit the province from which he took his title. The festival was to be held in the town hall of Angers.

With this letter came a personal invitation from the prince, who wrote that he remembered having seen my father formerly at the court of King Henri, and would be pleased to meet him again.

My first impulse was to entreat my father to decline, and I should certainly have persisted in my opposition if we had been invited by M. de Monsoreau alone; but my father feared a refusal of the prince's invitation might be viewed by his Highness as a mark of disrespect.

We went to the festival, then. M. de Monsoreau received us as if nothing had passed between us; his conduct in my regard was neither indifferent nor affected; he treated me just as he did the other ladies, and it gave me pleasure to find I was neither the object of his friendliness nor of his enmity.

But this was not the case with Duc d'Anjou. As soon as he saw me his eyes were riveted on me and never left me the rest of the evening. I felt ill at ease under his gaze, and without letting my father know my reason for wishing to retire from the ball, I urged him so strongly that we were the first to withdraw.

Three days later, M. de Monsoreau came to Méridor. I saw him at a distance coming up the avenue to the castle, and retired to my chamber.

I was afraid my father might summon me; but he did nothing of the kind, and, after half an hour, M. de Monsoreau left. No one had informed me of his visit, and my father never spoke of it; but I noticed that he was gloomier than usual after the departure of the deputy-governor.

Some days passed. One morning, after returning from a walk in the grounds, I was told M. de Monsoreau was with my father. The baron had inquired for me two or three times, and on each occasion seemed to be specially anxious as to the direction I had taken. He gave orders that my return should be at once announced to him.

And, in fact, I was hardly in my room when my father entered.

"My child," he said, "a motive which it is unnecessary you should be acquainted with compels me to send you away for a few days. Ask no questions; you must be sure that my motive must be very urgent, since it forces me to remain a week, a fortnight, perhaps even a month, without seeing you."

I shuddered, although unconscious of the danger to which I was exposed. But these two visits of M. de Monsoreau foreboded nothing good.

"But where am I to go, father?" I asked.

"To the Castle of Lude, to my sister, who will conceal you from every eye. It is necessary that the journey be made at night."

"Do you go with me?"

"No, I must stay here to divert suspicion; even the servants must not know where you are going."

"But who are to be my escort?"

"Two men upon whom I can rely."

"Oh, heavens! But father"—

The baron kissed me.

"My child," said he, "it cannot be helped."

I was so assured of my father's love that I made no further objection and asked for no explanation.

It was agreed between us that Gertrude, my nurse's daughter, should accompany me.

My father retired, after bidding me get ready.

We were in the long days of winter, and it was a very cold and dreary evening; at eight o'clock my father came for me. I was ready, as he had directed; we went downstairs noiselessly and crossed the garden; he opened a little door that led into the forest; there we found a litter waiting and two men. My father talked to them at length, apparently enjoining them to take great care of me. After this, I took my place in the litter, and Gertrude sat down beside me. The baron kissed me for the last time, and we started.

I was ignorant of the nature of the peril that threatened me and forced me to leave the Castle of Méridor. I questioned Gertrude, but she was quite as much in the dark as I was. I did not dare to ask information of my conductors, whom I did not know. We went along quietly by roundabout and devious paths, when, after travelling nearly two hours, at the very moment I was falling asleep, in spite of my anxiety, lulled by the smooth, monotonous motion of the litter, I was awakened by Gertrude, who seized me by the arm, as well as by the sudden stopping of the litter itself.

"Oh, mademoiselle!" cried the poor girl; "what is happening?"

I passed my head through the curtains; we were surrounded by six masked men on horseback; our own men, who had tried to defend us, were prisoners.

I was too frightened to call for help; besides, who would have answered my appeal? The man who appeared to be the leader of the band advanced to the litter.

"Do not be alarmed, mademoiselle," said he; "no harm is intended you, but you must follow us."

"Where?" I asked.

"To a place where so far from having any cause for fear, you will be treated as a queen."

This promise frightened me more than if he had threatened me.

"My father! oh, my father!" I murmured.

"Hear me, mademoiselle," whispered Gertrude. "I am acquainted with this neighborhood; you know I am devoted to you. I am strong; some misfortune will befall us if we do not escape."

The encouragement my poor maid was trying to give me was far from reassuring me. Still, it is comforting to know you have a friend when in trouble, and I felt a little relieved.

"Do as you like, gentlemen," I answered, "we are only two poor women and cannot resist."

One of the men dismounted, took the place of our conductor, and changed the direction of the litter. . . ."

We travelled nearly three hours; then the litter halted; I heard a door opening; some words were exchanged; the litter went on again, and, from the echoes that struck my ear, I concluded we were crossing a

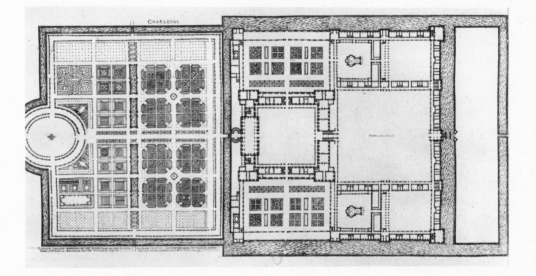

Engraving by Androuet de Cerceau of the château of Charleval and its vast formal gardens, the prototype for the famous gardens at Villandry château.

drawbridge. I was not mistaken; glancing through the curtains, I saw we were in the courtyard of a castle.

What castle was it? Neither Gertrude nor I could tell. We had often tried during the journey to find in what direction we were going, but all we were able to perceive was an endless forest. Both of us believed that the paths selected by our abductors were purposely circuitous, and designed to deprive us of any knowledge of where we were.

The door of our litter was opened and we were invited to alight by the same man that had spoken before.

I obeyed in silence. Two men, doubtless belonging to the castle, came with torches to receive us. In accordance with the alarming promise given to us before, we were treated with the greatest respect. We followed the men with the torches, and were conducted into a richly furnished bed-chamber, which had seemingly been furnished during the most elegant and brilliant period of the reign of François I.

A collation awaited us on a table sumptuously laid out.

"You are at home, madame," said the man who had already addressed me twice, "and as, of course, you require the services of a maid, yours will not leave; her room is next to your own."

Gertrude and I exchanged a look of relief.

"Every time you want anything," continued the masked man, "all you have to do is to strike the knocker of this door, and the man who is always on duty in the ante-chamber will be at your orders."

This apparent attention indicated that we would be kept in sight.

The masked man bowed and passed out, and we heard him double lock the door behind him.

And now we were alone, Gertrude and I.

For a moment we did not stir, but gazed into each other's eyes by the glare of the two candelabra which lit up the supper table. Gertrude wished to speak; I made her a sign to be silent; some one, perhaps, was listening.

The door of the room appointed for Gertrude was open; the same idea of visiting it occurred to both of us. She seized one of the candelabra, and we entered on tiptoe.

It was a large closet, evidently designed to serve as a dressing-room to the bed-chamber. It had another door, parallel to the one by which we had entered. This door was ornamented likewise with a little chiseled knocker of copper, which fell on a plate of the same metal, the whole so exquisitely wrought that it might have been the work of Benvenuto Cellini.

It was evident both doors opened into the same ante-chamber.

Gertrude brought the light close to the lock. The door was double-locked.

We were prisoners.

When two persons, though of different rank, are in the same situation and are partakers of the same perils, it is marvellous how quickly their ideas chime in together and how easily they pass beyond conventional phrases and useless words.

Gertrude approached me.

"Mademoiselle," she said in a low voice, "did you notice that, after we left the yard, we mounted only five steps?"

"Yes," I answered.

"Then we are on the ground floor?"

"Certainly."

"So that," she added, speaking still lower, and fastening her eyes on the outside shutters, "so that"—

"If these windows had no gratings"—I interrupted.

"Yes, and if madame had courage"—

"Courage!" I cried; "oh, rest easy, I'll have plenty of it, my child."

It was now Gertrude's turn to warn me to be silent.

"Yes, yes, I understand," said I.

Gertrude made me a sign to stay where I was, and returned to the bed-chamber with the candelabrum.

I had known already her meaning, and I went to the window and felt for the fastenings of the shutters.

I found them, or rather Gertrude did, and the shutters opened.

I uttered an exclamation of joy; the window was not grated.

But Gertrude had already noticed the cause of this seeming negligence of our jailers; a large pond bathed the foot of the wall; we were much better guarded by ten feet of water than we certainly could have been by grating on our windows.

However, on raising my eyes from the pond to the bank that enclosed it, I recognized a landscape that was familiar to me: we were prisoners in the Castle of Beaugé, where, as I have said before, I had often come with my father, and where I had been carried the day of my poor Daphne's death.

The Castle of Beaugé belonged to the Duc d'Anjou.

Then, as if a lightning flash had illumined my mind, I understood everything.

I gazed down into the water with gloomy satisfaction: it would be a last resource against violence, a last refuge from dishonor.

Twenty times during that night did I start up, a prey to unspeakable terrors; but nothing justified these terrors except the situation in which I was placed; nothing indicated that any one intended me harm; on the contrary, the whole castle seemed sunk in sleep, and only the cries of the birds in the marshes disturbed the silence of the night.

Daylight appeared, but though it dispelled the menacing aspect which darkness lends to the landscape, it but confirmed me in my fears during the night; flight was impossible without external aid, and where could such aid come from?

About nine there was a knock at our door; I passed into the room of Gertrude, telling her she might allow the persons who knocked to enter.

Those who knocked, as I could see from the closet, were the servants of the night before; they removed the supper, which we had not touched, and brought in breakfast.

Gertrude asked a few questions, but they passed out leaving them unanswered.

Then I returned. The reason of my presence in the Castle of Beaugé and of the pretended respect by which I was surrounded was explained. The Duc d'Anjou had seen me at the festival given by M. de Monsoreau; the Duc d'Anjou had fallen in love with me; my father, on learning of it, wished to save me from the pursuit of which I was doubtless to be the object. He had removed me from Méridor; but betrayed by a treacherous servant, or by an unfortunate accident, he had failed, and I had fallen into the hands of the man from whom he had vainly tried to deliver me.

I dwelt upon this explanation, the only one that was probable, and, in fact, the only one that was true.

Yielding to the entreaties of Gertrude, I drank a cup of milk and ate a bit of bread.

The morning passed in the discussion of wild plans of escape. About a hundred yards from us we could see a boat among the reeds with its oars; assuredly, if that boat had been within reach of us, my strength, intensified by my terror, would have sufficed, along with the natural strength of Gertrude, to extricate us from our captivity.

During this morning nothing occurred to alarm us. Dinner was served just as breakfast had been; I could hardly stand, I felt so weak. I sat down at table, waited on only by Gertrude, for our guardians retired as soon as they had placed the food on the table. But, just when I broke my loaf, I found a note inside of it. I opened it hurriedly; it contained but these few words:

"A friend is watching over you; you shall have news of him tomorrow, and of your father."

You can understand my joy; my heart beat as if it would burst through my breast. I showed Gertrude the note. The rest of the day was spent in waiting and hoping.

The second night slipped by as quietly as the first; then came the hour of breakfast, for which we had watched so impatiently; for I was sure I should find another note in my loaf.

I was not mistaken. The note was in these terms:

"The person who carried you off is coming to the Castle of Beaugé at ten o'clock tonight; but at nine, the friend who is watching over you will be under your window with a letter from your father, which will inspire you with that confidence in him which, perhaps, you might not otherwise feel.

"Burn this note."

I read this letter a second time and then threw it into the fire as I had been warned to do. The writing was completely unknown to me, and I confess I was ignorant where it came from.

Gertrude and I were lost in conjectures; we went to the window during the morning at least a hundred times in hope of seeing some one on the shore of the pond or in the depths of the forest; but we saw nothing.

An hour after dinner some one knocked at the door; it was the first time any one had attempted to come into our room except at meal-time; however, as we had no means of locking ourselves in, we were forced to tell the person he might enter.

It was the same man who had spoken to us at the litter and in the courtyard of the castle. I could not recognize him by his face, for he was masked at the time; but, at the first words he uttered, I recognized him by his voice.

He presented a letter.

"Whom do you come from, monsieur?" I asked.

"Have the goodness to read this letter, mademoiselle," said he, "and you will see."

"But I will not read the letter until I know from whom it comes."

"Mademoiselle, you are your own mistress. My orders were to hand you this letter. I shall lay it at your feet, and, if you deign to pick it up, you can do so."

And the servant, who was apparently an equerry, to make good his words, placed the letter on the cushion upon which I rested my feet, and passed out.

"What is to be done?" I asked Gertrude.

"The advice I should take the liberty of offering, mademoiselle, would be to open this letter. It may warn us against some peril, and we may be the better prepared to escape it."

The advice was reasonable; I abandoned my first intention, and opened the letter.

ALEXANDRE DUMAS
The Lady of Monsoreau, 1846

CHAMBORD, THE INSOLUBLE LABYRINTH

Henry James was already widely regarded as the greatest living practitioner of the novel when, in 1884, he brought his exceptional eye for detail and his consummate craftsmanship to bear on a travelog deceptively entitled A Little Tour in France. *"We good Americans," James noted in his introduction, "are too apt to think that France is Paris." This, he hastened to add, "is by no means the case. . . . It had already been intimated to the author of these light pages that there are many good things in the* doux pays de France *of which you get no hint in a walk between those ornaments of the capital." The sweet countryside of France—specifically the region around Chambord—is the subject of the following excerpt.*

The second time I went to Blois I took a carriage for Chambord, and came back by the Château de Cheverny and the forest of Russy,—a charming little expedition, to which the beauty of the afternoon (the finest in a rainy season that was spotted with bright days) contributed not a little. To go to Chambord, you cross the Loire, leave it on one side, and strike away through a country in which salient features become less and less numerous, and which at last has no other quality than a look of intense and peculiar rurality,—the characteristic, even when it is not the charm, of so much of the landscape of France. This is not the appearance of wildness, for it goes with great cultivation; it is simply the presence of the delving, drudging, economizing peasant. But it is a deep, unrelieved rusticity. It is a peasant's landscape; not, as in England, a landlord's. On the way to Chambord you enter the flat and sandy Sologne. The wide horizon opens out like a great *potager*, without interruptions, without an eminence, with here and there a long, low stretch of wood. There is an absence of hedges, fences, signs of property; everything is absorbed in the general flatness—the patches of vineyard, the scattered cottages, the villages, the children (planted and staring and almost always pretty), the women in the fields, the white caps, the faded blouses, the big sabots. At the end of an hour's drive (they assure you at Blois that even with two horses you will spend double that time), I passed through a sort of gap in a wall, which does duty as the gateway of the domain of an exiled pretender. I drove along a straight avenue, through a disfeatured park,— the park of Chambord has twenty-one miles of circumference,—a very sandy, scrubby, melancholy plantation, in which the timber must have been cut many times over and is today a mere tangle of brushwood. Here, as in so many spots in France, the traveller perceives that he is in a land of revolutions. Nevertheless, its great extent and the long perspective of its avenues give this desolate boskage a certain majesty; just as its shabbiness places it in agreement with one of the strongest impressions of the château. You follow one of these long perspectives a proportionate time, and at last you see the chimneys and pinnacles of Chambord rise apparently out of the ground. The filling-in of the wide moats that formerly surrounded it has, in vulgar parlance, let it down, and given it an appearance of top-heaviness that is at the same time a magnificent Orientalism. The towers, the turrets, the cupolas, the gables, the lanterns, the chimneys, look more like the spires of a city than the salient points of a single building. You emerge from the avenue and find yourself at the foot of an enormous fantastic mass. Chambord has a strange mixture of society and solitude. A little village clusters within view of its stately windows, and a couple of inns near by offer entertainment to pilgrims. These things, of course, are incidents of the political proscription which hangs its thick veil over the place. Chambord is truly royal,—royal in its great scale, its grand air, its indifference to common considerations. If a cat may look at a king, a palace may look at a tavern. I enjoyed my visit to this extraordinary structure as much as if I had been a legitimist; and indeed there is something interesting in any monument of a great system, any bold presentation of a tradition.

You leave your vehicle at one of the inns, which are very decent and tidy, and in which every one is very civil, as if in this latter respect the influence of the old régime pervaded the neighborhood, and you walk across the grass and the gravel to a small door,—a door infinitely subordinate and conferring no title of any kind on those who enter it. Here you ring a bell, which a highly respectable person answers (a person perceptibly affiliated, again, to the old regimé), after which she ushers you across a vestibule into an inner court. Perhaps the strongest impression I got at Chambord came to me as I stood in this court. The woman who admitted me did not come with me; I was to find my guide somewhere else. The specialty of Chambord is its prodigious round towers. There are, I believe, no less than eight of them, placed at each angle of the inner and outer square of buildings; for the castle is in the form of a larger structure which encloses a smaller one. One of these towers stood before me in the court; it seemed to fling its shadow over the place; while above, as I looked up, the pinnacles and gables, the enormous chimneys, soared into the bright blue air. The place was empty and silent; shadows of gargoyles, of extraordinary projections, were thrown across the clear gray surfaces. One felt that the whole thing was monstrous. A cicerone appeared, a languid young man in a rather shabby livery, and led me about with a mixture of the impatient and the desultory, of condescension and humility. I do not profess to understand the plan of Chambord, and I may add that I do not even desire to do so; for it is much more entertaining to think of it, as you can so easily, as an irresponsible, insoluble labyrinth. Within, it is a wilderness of empty chambers, a royal and romantic barrack. The exiled prince to whom it gives its title has not the means to keep up four hundred rooms; he contents himself with preserving the huge outside. The repairs of the prodigious roof alone must absorb a large part of his revenue. The great feature of the interior is the celebrated double staircase, rising straight through the building, with two courses of steps, so that people may ascend and descend without meeting. This staircase is a truly majestic piece of humor; it gives you the note, as it were, of Chambord. It opens on each landing to a vast guard-room, in four arms, radiations of the winding shaft. My guide made me climb to the great open-work lantern which, springing from the roof at the termination of the rotund staircase (surmounted here by a smaller one), forms the pinnacle of the bristling crown of Chambord. This lantern is tipped with a huge *fleur-de-lis* in stone,—the only one, I believe, that the Revolution did not succeed in pulling down. Here, from narrow windows, you look over the wide, flat country and the tangled, melancholy park, with the rotation of its straight avenues. Then you walk about the roof, in a complication of galleries, terraces, balconies, through the multitude of chimneys and gables. This roof, which is in itself a sort of castle in the air, has an extravagant, fabulous quality, and with its profuse ornamentation,—the salamander of

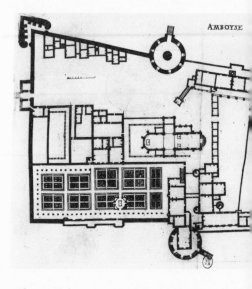

The quondam royal residence, Amboise: above, a floorplan showing gardens and towers; below, the hall in which the Estates General met, emblazoned with the royal fleurs-de-lis.

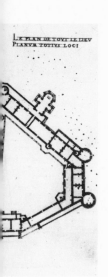

Francis I is constant motive,—its lonely pavements, its sunny niches, the balcony that looks down over the closed and grass-grown main entrance, a strange, half-sad, half-brilliant charm. The stone-work is covered with fine mould. There are places that reminded me of some of those quiet, mildewed corners of courts and terraces, into which the traveller who wanders through the Vatican looks down from neglected windows. They show you two or three furnished rooms, with Bourbon portraits, hideous tapestries from the ladies of France, a collection of the toys of the *enfant du miracle*, all military and of the finest make. "Tout cela fonctionne," the guide said of these miniature weapons; and I wondered, if he should take it into his head to fire off his little cannon, how much harm the Comte de Chambord would do.

From below, the castle would look crushed by the redundancy of its upper protuberances if it were not for the enormous girth of its round towers, which appear to give it a robust lateral development. These towers, however, fine as they are in their way, struck me as a little stupid; they are the exaggeration of an exaggeration. In a building erected after the days of defence, and proclaiming its peaceful character from its hundred embroideries and cupolas, they seem to indicate a want of invention. I shall risk the accusation of bad taste if I say that, impressive as it is, the Château de Chambord seemed to me to have altogether a little of that quality of stupidity. The trouble is that it represents nothing very particular; it has not happened, in spite of sundry vicissitudes, to have a very interesting history. Compared with that of Blois and Amboise, its past is rather vacant; and one feels to a certain extent the contrast between its pompous appearance and its spacious but somewhat colorless annals. It had indeed the good fortune to be erected by Francis I, whose name by itself expresses a good deal of history. Why he should have built a palace in those sandy plains will ever remain an unanswered question, for kings have never been obliged to give reasons. In addition to the fact that the country was rich in game and that Francis was a passionate hunter, it is suggested by M. de la Saussaye, the author of the very complete little history of Chambord which you may buy at the bookseller's at Blois, that he was governed in his choice of the site by the accident of a charming woman having formerly lived there. The Comtesse de Thoury had a manor in the neighborhood, and the Comtesse de Thoury had been the object of a youthful passion on the part of the most susceptible of princes before his accession to the throne. This great pile was reared, therefore, according to M. de la Saussaye, as a *souvenir de premières amours!* It is certainly a very massive memento; and if these tender passages were proportionate to the building that commemorates them, they were tender indeed. There has been much discussion as to the architect employed by Francis I, and the honor of having designed this splendid residence has been claimed for several of the Italian artists who early in the sixteenth century came to seek patronage in France. It seems well established to-day, however, that Chambord was the work neither of Primaticcio, of Vignola, nor of Il Rosso, all of whom have left some trace of their sojourn in France; but of an obscure yet very complete genius, Pierre Nepveu, known as Pierre Trinqueau, who is designated in the papers which preserve in some degree the history of the origin of the edifice, as the *maistre de l'oeuvre de maçonnerie*. Behind this modest title, apparently, we must recognize one of the most original talents of the French Renaissance; and it is a proof of the vigor of the artistic life of that period that, brilliant production being everywhere abundant, an artist of so high a value should not have been treated by his contemporaries as a celebrity. We manage things very differently to-day. . . .

On the whole, Chambord makes a great impression; and the hour I was there, while the yellow afternoon light slanted upon the September woods, there was a dignity in its desolation. It spoke, with a muffled but audible voice, of the vanished monarchy, which had been so strong, so splendid, but to-day has become a sort of fantastic vision, like the cupolas and chimneys that rose before me. I thought, while I lingered there, of all the fine things it takes to make up such a monarchy; and how one of them is a superfluity of mouldering, empty palaces. Chambord is touching,—that is the best word for it; and if the hopes of another restoration are in the follies of the Republic, a little reflection on that eloquence of ruin ought to put the Republic on its guard. A sentimental tourist may venture to remark that in the presence of several châteaux which appeal in this mystical manner to the retrospective imagination, it cannot afford to be foolish.

HENRY JAMES
A Little Tour in France, 1885

THE BRETON DUCHESS

Anne de Bretagne's marriage to Charles VIII of France, celebrated in the great hall of the château of Langeais in December of 1491, added Brittany to the holdings of the French crown. But as this description of Anne—excerpted from Theodore Cook's Old Touraine, The Life and History of the Famous Châteaux of France—*makes abundantly clear, the bride had more to offer than her Breton landholdings. Her "small and delicate figure"—and her widely acknowledged beauty—account at least in part for the avidness with which Charles' successor, Louis XII, wooed Anne after her first husband's untimely death in 1498.*

We had already heard much of Anne de Bretagne in the course of our wanderings along the Loire, and after seeing her oratory at Loches it became impossible to put off any longer a visit to the hall where she was married in Langeais. The road from Tours to Langeais is a straight and good one, whether for riding or driving, and follows the right or north bank of the river past Luynes to Cinq Mars, where the railway crosses over too, and follows the road into Langeais between the river and a hill upon its banks.

The village at first sight does not look attractive, but there is one good main street, from which numberless little alleys open out lined by tiny cottages, and ending in a strip of green or garden fround. At the end of the street rise two vast round towers that from a distance look far too big for their surroundings, and it is not till the visitor is fairly in the little square beyond the house of Rabelais, and face to face with the main entrance, that he can realise the full proportions of the Château of Langeais.

Alingavia, says M. Mabille, was one of the oldest of the Roman settlements, and Roman remains are still traceable in the foundations of the old donjon keep, rebuilt in 1000. Gregory of Tours tells us, too, that St.

Martin built a church here, and the present edifice contains some of the early work near the east end, which is triapsal; some old shafts and arches are arranged on the south side so as to form a covered walk externally.

But of the buildings within the castle walls, of which distinct traces are still left, the fort built by Foulques Nerra to blockade Eudes at Tours is the oldest. Little but the outer shell of its walls and a few traces of masonry about the windows remain, but from the little hill on which it stands can be obtained the finest view of the inner side of the château. "The interior court"—I quote from Mrs. Mark Pattison—"is almost wholly confined by the buildings around it; the high walls which defend it on the outside are cut up at well-guarded angles by massive towers, and pierced at irregular intervals by narrow openings. The whole length is crowned by heavy machicolated battlements, so that the aspect of the exterior is severe, but the façade which looks upon the court is not wanting in elegance. Four small towers, each of which contains a spiral staircase, break the monotony of the front and give access to the different stories. The interior space is divided out in the simplest fashion, and the arrangements adopted on the ground floor continue in unvarying repetition tier above tier. But above, along the roof, run no heavy battlements; a bold projecting cornice takes their place in surmounting the wall, and over this rises a sharply pointed roof, the outline of which is broken by towers and pierced by chimneys and dormers."

I have quoted thus far to make quite clear the exact position of Langeais in the architecture of Touraine. It is a fortress of the Middle Ages that is one of the finest existing examples of a French castle built about the middle of the fifteenth century, and bears upon its very walls the traces of coming change. The cornice, which at Langeais replaces the battlements on the walls of the inside only, is destined soon to replace them on the outside also. "At Chenonceaux, at Azay-le-Rideau, at Blois, at Chambord, its bold projecting lines encircle each building with a crown." We had seen the older forms of feudal architecture at Chinon and at Loches; Langeais seemed the connecting link between the older order and the new. The problem which its architect had to solve was to combine a stronghold capable of defense with a house calculated for the increasing necessities of daily life; the fortifications seem planned on a scale very much behind the science of the times, for gunpowder is left wholly out of the calculation, while every means for keeping out an escalade attack has been carefully made use of: the only gate that opens from without into the court is flanked, as at Chaumont, by two massive towers and guarded by a portcullis.

Of the first building on this site, after the Black Count's donjon had fallen into ruins, little save a few bricks remains to indicate that Romano-Gallic methods of construction still continued. A later château was begun by Pierre de la Brosse, the son of a good family in Touraine, who had seen some service in the Court of St. Louis, and reached the highest powers of a favorite under Philip III. Against all the enemies whom such a position naturally aroused Pierre was able to make a good resistance until he imprudently attacked the reputation of the Queen, who joined the barons against him and finally hanged him at Vincennes in 1272, on charges which have remained unknown and were probably designedly obscured.

It is this same old château which was occupied by the English during their invasions while the Black Prince was making his campaign along the Loire; it was given up to Charles VII, only to be retaken, and at last the English were bought out of Langeais as they were out of Rochecorbon by the combined subsidies of the citizens of Touraine.

The Château of Langeais as it stands at present was built in 1464 under the direction of Jean Briçonnet, first mayor of Tours, by the care of Jean Bourree, minister of Louis XI, and governor of Langeais, who was also the builder of Plessis-lez-Tours, a château which in its complete state was very like what Langeais has remained. The place is now in the possession of M. Siegfried, and, by his judicious and tasteful expenditure of large sums of money, is being gradually brought into one harmonious picture of oak carvings, tapestry, and warm tiled floors—the chimney and ceiling of the Salle des Gardes are especially beautiful; its walls are painted by Lameire with the arms of Anne de Bretagne, whose cordelière reappears in many other details of the decoration.

Perhaps the strangest feature of the place is the quaint little passage beneath the roof, the guards' "chemin de ronde," formed by the machicolations, that extends all round the château, lighted by innumerable little windows which give an ever-changing view of the valley of the Loire from the forest of Chinon west and south, to the cathedral towers of Tours far off among the mist towards the east. But the most interesting room in Langeais is the great hall, where Anne de Bretagne was married to King Charles VIII of France.

The story of the war in Brittany, and the revolt of Orleans against the Regent Anne de Beaujeu, has already introduced us to the little Breton duchess. Brantôme sketches her portrait in his Gallery of Illustrious Ladies. "Her figure," says he, "was small and delicate. It is true that one leg was shorter than the other, though by very little, and it was scarcely noticeable, for her beauty was no whit damaged by that. . . . Besides, there would seem to be a great fascination about the walk of such women, owing to certain graces of movement which are not commonly found in others." Add to this a calm and dignified carriage, which revealed the firm will and resolution of character ripened at an early age by the troubles of the times. But if Anne had thus far gained from her Breton upbringing, she had all the Breton faults, the pride, the anger, and the self-will of that strong and narrowed nationality. If her wishes were clearly defined, her will imperious, her views were also somewhat limited: she lacked the supple nature of a truly great woman, because she was without that loftiness of mind and intellect which allows its possessor to appreciate while it criticizes every form of life and manners with which it comes in contact. This is why we find her alternately the prey to pride, to anger, and to hate, to a tenacity of purpose through good and evil which degenerates into a wrong-headed sullenness. "Once she has bethought her of anything," says Contarini, the Venetian ambassador, "she must have her way, whether by smiles or tears." Similarly it is her love of vengeance, her unrelenting hatred, that her panegyrist Brantôme can alone find to blame. . . .

A princess with so strongly marked a character was not one to let herself be married at the convenience of her subjects or of any man, and all Europe had been already somewhat amused at her capture of the unwilling Maximilian and her alliance with England and Spain. This could have but one result. Anne's new allies were by no means inclined to attach the importance to the Breton duchess which she desired, and France was only made the more attentive to the frontier and the incessant quarrels of the Breton lords. At last the politic and skilful Regent saw her opportunity. Making every use of the influence over Anne possessed by the young Duke of Orleans just released from prison, and tempting at the same time her ambition by the offer of a throne, the Regent arranged the marriage of her younger brother Charles VIII with the heiress of Brittany. The duchess had little scruple in giving up her tardy lover Maximilian, whose daughter had already been somewhat similarly abandoned by the King of France, and in December 1491 the marriage contract of Anne and Charles VIII was drawn up in the great hall of the Château of Langeais, which assured the union of France and Brittany, and gave the business-like little Breton the right of marrying the next King of France if she outlived her first husband.

THEODORE ANDREA COOK
Old Touraine, 1906

The vaulted gallery surrounding the sunlit cloister of Fontevrault abbey.

Joan of Arc has had many biographers but few more extraordinary in their own right than Victoria Sackville-West, descendant of the sixteenth-century English poet, dramatist, and statesman Thomas Sackville and wife of Harold Nicolson, biographer, historian, and diplomat. Already an acclaimed poet and novelist by the mid-1930s—which happened to mark the middle of her career as well—Sackville-West turned to hagiography, producing first Saint Joan of Arc *and then a life of Stes. Teresa of Avila and Thérèse of Lisieux. This passage from her life of Joan finds the "Pucelle of Domremy," as the warrior-maid was known, en route to the besieged city of Orléans.*

Two views of Chenonceaux: above, the long gallery added by Catherine de Médicis to span the Cher; at right, the vestibule with its ceiling of royal escutcheons.

On Friday, April 29th, 1429, the news spread in Orleans that a force, led by the Pucelle of Domremy, was on its way to the relief of the city, a piece of news which, as the chronicler remarks, comforted them greatly.

The army had, in fact, left Blois on the 27th, the priests going ahead intoning the *Veni Creator Spiritus*, the long train of horsemen, men-at-arms, waggons, and four hundred head of cattle stringing out along the road behind them. It was a great moment for Jeanne. She had got her forces at last—three to four thousand men following her. Jean de Metz and Poulengy were still with her; they were familiar companions; they had believed in her from the first—they had accompanied her on that precarious journey from Vaucouleurs to Chinon. On that journey, they had ridden on either side of her horse in the desire to escort and protect her; then, she was nothing but a girl dependent upon their chivalry; now, she was officially the envoy of the Dauphin, as well as the self-appointed envoy of the Lord. Her brothers had joined her too: Pierre and Jean, those same brothers who had been told by their father to drown their sister rather than allow her to "go with soldiers." Besides these, she had some of the most distinguished names of France in her company; she was riding in the midst of famous captains: the maréchal de Sainte-Sévère; the maréchal de Rais; Louis de Culen, Admiral of France; Ambroise de Loré; and the formidable Gascon, Etienne de Vignolles, known as La Hire.

Although she was not actually in command of the army, as is frequently and erroneously supposed, but was merely under the escort of these men, she conducted herself from the first in her usual high-handed manner. She interfered with them, not on military but on personal grounds. First she made them all go to confession, and then decreed that all their loose women should be left behind, two edicts which must have astonished them considerably, but which they nevertheless obeyed. She had them all under her control, the only woman now left riding with those thousands of rough men, not even officially their leader. La Hire, least tractable of soldiers, was forced to forgo his habit of violent swearing, though as a concession he was allowed to use Jeanne's own two favourite exclamations: *en nom Dieu* and *par mon martin!*—which must, to him, have seemed very like a cup of milk to a man pining for strong drink. La Hire emerges out of the crowd as a definite personality. Whatever we know of him is all very much of a piece. His oaths and his prayers fit together. He swore and he prayed. When he prayed, his prayer was almost in the nature of an oath, it was almost in the nature of a threat to God. . . .

They slept in the fields, the first night on the way from Blois. Jeanne, unaccustomed to the weight of the armour which she refused to remove,

awoke bruised and weary. But they were drawing nearer to Orleans and the spirit counted for more than the body. The second night, that is, Thursday 28th, they encamped opposite the Ile Saint Loup, little more than a mile beyond Orleans, on the south bank of the Loire. It was then that Jeanne discovered that she had been, as she thought, tricked. A great deal of ink has been spilt in trying to decide how far and how intentionally the captains had tricked her; for my own part I do not believe that they had intended to trick her at all. . . .

Blois and Orleans both lie on the Loire with a distance of thirty-four miles between them. Orleans, however, lay entirely on the north bank; therefore in order to arrive there from Blois, the army had two alternative routes: the one on the north side, which would have allowed them to approach the city without having to cross the river; the other on the south side, which would entail the use of boats and bridges. On the face of it, it seems inexplicable that the captains should have chosen the south side, with the dangerous necessity of transporting a large force and all their supplies by a water-way involving slow sailing-boats or pontoon-bridges linking the opposite shores with the help of sandy islets. Still, choose it they did, and on her arrival Jeanne to her great disgust found herself with the river between herself and her enemies. There were reasons, of course, for a choice which otherwise seems so inexplicable, and those reasons may be very briefly stated by saying that the English positions were far stronger and more numerous on the north, west, and south sides than on the east, and that in the neighborhood of the Ile Saint Loup, where the army was brought to a halt, the English positions were especially weak. What strikes us as odd is that they should not have explained their reasons quite simply to Jeanne when they saw her beginning to get into one of her tempers. Why, after all, should they have wanted to trick her, once having accepted her as their hope and their salvation? If she had really expected to be led through la Beauce (that is to say, on the north side), instead of through la Sologne (on the south), why on earth should they not have trusted her with the reasons for their decision? Was it because they regarded her as a religious inspiration rather than as a military commander? She held, after all, no official command. Was it because, haughtily but not unnaturally, these experienced captains saw no obligation to admit this totally inexperienced girl into their councils, although they were quite prepared to indulge her whims by going to confession on her demand and even by dismissing the disreputable women from their ranks? Was it because they regarded her as a sort of mascot rather than as a soldier like themselves? Was it merely because they already knew the danger of entering into argument with so intransigent a personality and thought the only chance of keeping her quiet was to keep her in the dark? Or was it that Jeanne herself had displayed no interest whatsoever in her route, being by now confident that she was being led straight towards Talbot and his English? Was it, finally, because they regarded themselves less as a relieving force than as an armed escort to the valuable provisions they were taking to the necessitous Orleans? They were, undeniably, so much encumbered that they could scarcely have risked a sudden swoop from the English on the road through la Beauce. The road through la Sologne, though less heroic, was much safer. I think any, or several, of these explanations may be true. But that they deliberately tricked her with malicious intent I find hard to believe.

Jeanne, however, was very angry indeed. It was pouring with rain; it was a stormy day; it was late; she was tired; her armour hurt her; and she was disappointed. She had expected to find herself under the very walls of Orleans, with nothing but the English between her and the accomplishment of her dream, instead of which these men whom she had trusted had landed her on the wrong side of a large river, with, so far as she could see, nothing but further delays and difficulties in her way. The Bastard of Orleans, hastily crossing the river in a small boat to greet her on her arrival—for he was as anxious to see her as were the people of Orleans—met with a very poor reception. Jeanne was no respecter of persons. It did not affect her in the least that the Bastard should be in command of the very city she had come to relieve; that his goodwill should be of such vital importance to her; that he should be of royal blood, the first cousin of her own Dauphin, the half-brother of her especial charge the captive Duke of Orleans, and the half-uncle by

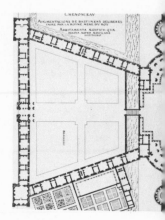

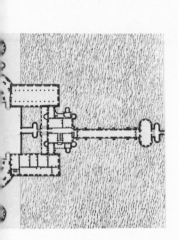

marriage of her beloved Alençon; that he should already be the Bastard of Orleans, whereas she was not yet its Pucelle. Nor did she stop to reflect that it was very gracious of him to come in person to receive her. Her opening words to him were anything but gracious. He himself has left a report of them. "Jeanne spoke in the following terms: 'Is it you who are the Bastard of Orleans?' 'I am, and I rejoice in your arrival.' Then she said, 'Is it you who advised them to bring me here by this bank of the river, instead of sending me straight to Talbot and his English?' I replied that I, and others wiser than myself, had given this advice, believing it to be the best and wisest. Then Jeanne spoke in these terms, *'En nom Dieu!* the counsel of Our Lord is wiser and better than yours. You thought to deceive me, but you have deceived yourselves, for I bring you the finest help that ever was brought to knight or to city, since it is the help of the King of Heaven.' "

The poor Bastard must have been in great perplexity. The whole of Orleans was feverishly awaiting the Maid, and he could not afford to alienate her. Besides, he himself believed in her; was it not largely due to his efforts that she had arrived at Orleans at all? And, now that she had arrived, he confronted no soft saintly girl, but a stern and angry young captain with very definite ideas of her own. Luckily, as soon appears from subsequent events, he was possessed of a certain instinctive skill in managing her. He needed all the skill he possessed, for there were complications which Jeanne had not taken into consideration; which nobody, indeed, could have taken into consideration unless they had been familiar with the place, or furnished with excellent maps, or in close and constant touch with those upon the spot. Jeanne had enjoyed none of these advantages; it is far more probable that she had formed no practical idea of Orleans at all before arriving there, and had thought of it in her simple faith as a second Jericho whose walls would fall before the trumpet-blast of her Lord. She had made some such declaration at Poitiers, saying that the siege would be raised and the city liberated after she had made her demand in the name of God. The Bastard took a more practical view. He had formed a plan which in appearance was a sound and simple one. He had intended to borrow boats from the citizens and to sail them up-stream as far as Chécy, a village on the north bank about five miles distant from Orleans. The cattle and provisions were meanwhile to await the arrival of the boats opposite Chécy, and were to be fetched by them on the following morning, when they were to be transported across the river and driven down towards Orleans, entering the town by the east gate or Porte de Bourgogne. This side of the town was the least strongly defended, as can readily be seen by . . . reference to the map. The English held only one fort on that side, the Bastille de Saint Loup, and it had been calculated that the French garrison, issuing from the Porte de Bourgogne with the support of the citizens, would suffice to hold the garrison of Saint Loup in check while the train of cattle passed into the town. It reads almost from the Bastard's account, as though he had no thought of attempting actually to relieve the town by force of arms until he had been able to re-victual it, a sensible and prudent course which, at best, could not have accorded at all with Jeanne's ideas. Unfortunately for the Bastard, even this sensible and prudent course went wrong. It went wrong for two reasons.

For one thing, he and his fellow-commanders were forced to the conclusion that the relieving force which had just arrived was wholly inadequate to oppose the English resistance. For another thing, and far more importantly, it proved impossible to take the boats up the river. The wind was blowing in the wrong direction. That was a factor beyond all human calculation or control.

They tried to explain this to Jeanne. She would only reply by telling them to wait a little, all would be well. And suddenly, inexplicably, the wind changed.

In spite of this dramatic event, which enabled them to pass the English fort and up the river in safety, Jeanne's difficulties were not yet at an end. True, her reputation had gone up at a bound, for her prophecy about the wind had very naturally impressed the Bastard and his friends, but there still remained the practical obstacle that the army was not considered sufficient to encounter the English in battle. Indeed, it seems unlikely that either the Bastard or the captains had ever regarded it otherwise than as a convoy for the cattle and the waggons. Having accomplished its mission, the Bastard wanted it to return to Blois. At the same time, he wanted Jeanne to stay behind and to accompany him into Orleans. Orleans was very anxious to see Jeanne. Now that the sails were filled with wind, he begged her to cross the Loire with him and the Grand-Prior of France, Nicolas de Giresme. This suggestion seems to have upset her considerably, and for the most unexpected reason. It was not that she resented the dismissal of her army; it was not that she feared that their disappearance would diminish her chance of relieving Orleans; no, she seems to have forgotten all about Orleans at the moment, and to have thought only of her own reluctance to separate herself from her troops, who were all confessed, repentant, and animated by good feelings. Really, what a strange character the Bastard must have thought her! Here she was within reach of Orleans at last; having worried Baudricourt, the Dauphin, and the Court of Poitiers into allowing her to go there; having spoken in and out of season of her divine mission to relieve the town; having even induced the elements to alter their arrangements in order to oblige her, and now she only wanted to go away again, all because she refused to be separated from an army which she had persuaded into a state of grace! What could the Bastard have made of such a girl? Certainly his opinion of her religious convictions may have grown, but he cannot have thought any better of her as a military authority. Curiously enough, the captains who had brought her all that way seemed equally reluctant to part with her; the Bastard had to beg and require of them that they should allow her to enter Orleans, while they themselves returned to Blois, crossed the river by the bridge there, and made their way back to Orleans by the northern road. His diplomacy succeeded; he got the captains to add their persuasion to his—"Jeanne," they said, "go in surety, for we promise to return to you before long," and Jeanne finally also relented, coming towards him with her standard in her hand. They crossed and spent the night at Chécy. It was his first experience of managing his saint, but not the last; a few days later she was telling him that she would have his head off if he did not do as she demanded.

VICTORIA SACKVILLE-WEST
Saint Joan of Arc, 1936

REFERENCE

A Chronology of the Loire

52 B.C.	Vercingetorix, chief of the Arverin Celts and leader of the Gauls, launches his campaign against Julius Caesar from the Celtic capitals of Tours and Orléans
A.D. 371	St. Martin named bishop of Tours
397	Death of St. Martin in the village of Candes; as his body is borne to Tours for burial, Loire valley experiences first "St. Martin's summer"
507	Clovis, leader of the Franks, marches against the Visigoths, kills their king, Alaric, and drives the remaining barbarians south across the Pyrenees
573	Death of Euphronius, bishop of Tours, who is succeeded by his nephew, Georgius Florentius, later known as St. Gregory of Tours
732	Charles Martel defeats Saracens at Tours, driving invaders back to Spain and ending epoch of Arab incursions into Western Europe
768	King Pepin the Short dies of fever and is succeeded by his ambitious son, Charlemagne
800	Charlemagne crowned emperor in Rome; Théodulf, abbot of St. Benedict and friend of Charlemagne, founds Germigny-des-Prés, held to be the oldest rural church in France; Alcuin, a noted scholar, is invited to leave York, England, and settle at Charlemagne's court; he founds *scriptoria* at a number of Loire valley monasteries, notably St. Benoît
814	Charlemagne dies at age of seventy-two
843	Frankland divided among Charlemagne's heirs; Loire goes to his grandson Charles the Bald
867	Despite the valiant efforts of Robert le Fort, count of Blois and progenitor of the Capetian kings of France, Normans captures Angers
873	Charles le Chauve recaptures Angers by rerouting the Maine river into a canal, rendering the Norman fleet of shallow-draft *drakkars* useless
987	Louis V, last of the Carolingian line, dies childless; crown offered to Hugh Capet, a descendant of Robert le Fort and one of the greatest landowners in the central Loire valley
1004	Fulk the Black founds the abbey of Beaulieu-les-Loches to house a fragment of Christ's tomb
1010	Creation of St. Peter's abbey of Solesmes, where Benedictines later rediscover Gregorian chants
1040	Geoffroy Martel, count of Anjou, founds abbey of the Trinity in Vendôme; Fulk the Black dies
1066	On the ruins of abbey of Fleury, construction of abbey of St. Benoît-sur-Loire begins; building continues intermittently until 1218
1099	Creation of the Fontevrault order, whose abbesses are almost always the daughters of kings
1104	Council of Beaugency excommunicates Phillippe I for running away with Bertrade, wife of the count of Anjou, but cannot prevent the king's eventual burial in vaults at St. Benoît
1119	William, son of Henry I of England, marries Matilda, daughter of Fulk V; thereafter, Henry's daughter Maud marries Fulk's son Geoffrey
1131	Count Fulk, now married to daughter of the king of Jerusalem, is crowned king
1144	Upon the death of Henry I, Geoffrey invades Normandy and is crowned duke
1149	Duchy of Normandy turned over to Geoffrey's son, Henry, who is but sixteen years old
1152	Second Council of Beaugency annuls the marriage of Louis VII and Eleanor of Aquitaine, who promptly marries Henry, Duke of Normandy and Count of Anjou
1154	Following the death of his uncle, King Stephen, Henry succeeds to the English throne
1183	Henry and Eleanor lose their firstborn son, Prince Henry, to dysentery; another son, Geoffrey, dies from wounds received in a jousting tournament
1189	Henry II dies at Chinon while campaigning against his surviving sons, Richard and John; the former, nicknamed the Lion-Hearted, becomes Richard I
1199	Richard dies at Chalus of blood poisoning from a wound received during the siege of Loches; John becomes king in his stead; the great abbey of Fontevrault built with crypt for Plantagenets
1202	King John captures Mirebeau, releases Queen Eleanor, and captures Arthur of Brittany, who dies under mysterious circumstances while in John's custody
1204	Eleanor of Aquitaine dies at age of eighty-two
1205	Loches, wrested from John's hands by his enemies, is converted into a state prison
1212	John loses control of his holdings in France and retreats to England; his half-brother, William, is defeated by King Philip at Bournes
1216	Death of King John; Philip confiscates his French possessions; Loire valley returns to French crown
1220	Isabelle, John's widow, marries Hugh le Brun, Lord of Lusignan and Count of La Marche
1230–40	Construction of Angers castle
1246	Isabelle's corpse buried at Fontevrault
1341	Death of Duke of Brittany marks the beginning of conflict known as the Hundred Years' War
1355	The Black Prince lands at Bordeaux; a year later he captures King John II of France
1360	Treaty of Bretigny
1364	John II dies and is succeeded by Charles V
1380	Death of Charles V; succession of Charles VI
1391	Louis d'Orléans, brother of Charles VI, buys the château of Blois with money obtained from the wife of the castle's rightful owner
1413	Edward III's grandson crowned Henry V of England; Henry promptly declares himself King of France as well
1415	Henry's army victorious at Agincourt, "the most disgraceful event that ever happened in the Kingdom of France," one chronicler calls battle
1419	Henry V conquers all of Normandy; Treaty of Troyes, signed one year later, makes Henry heir and regent of France, displacing Charles VI's son, the Dauphin

1422	Henry dies at age thirty-four and is succeeded by his infant son, Henry VI
1425	Dauphin crowned Charles VII as Joan of Arc, age thirteen, hears voices directing her to assist the new king
1427	Charles VII settles at Chinon, where Joan is presented to him two years later
1429	Joan of Arc raises English seige of Orléans, then goes to Sully to rejoin Charles and bring him to Reims to be crowned; captured by the English, Joan is burned at the stake as a heretic
1443–53	Jacques Coeur, treasurer of Charles VII, builds a palace at Bourges for 100,000 écus d'or
1453	End of the Hundred Years' War
1461	Louis XI crowned king
1465–1510	Construction of Chaumont by Pierre d'Amboise
1466–69	Louis XI orders construction of Langeais
1468–73	Jean Bourré, treasurer to Louis XI, builds castle of Plessis-Bourré
1472	Louis XI countermands d'Amboise's order to dismantle Chaumont and aids in its restoration
1483	Louis XI dies at Plessis-le-Tours; Charles VIII becomes king at age thirteen
1484	Reconstruction of castle of Gien, which has overlooked the Loire since age of Charlemagne
1491	Charles VIII marries Anne of Brittany at Langeais; he orders the construction of a palace-fortress at Amboise
1496	Charles dies childless and is succeeded by his cousin, Louis XII, son of the duke d'Orléans
1498	Louis XII receives the papal legate, César Borgia, at Chinon; his marriage to Jeanne, daughter of Louis XI, dissolved, the king marries Anne; they add St. Calais chapel to Blois
1512–21	Thomas Bohier, tax collector for Louis XII, buys Chenonceaux, razes existing castle except for one tower, and builds present structure
1514	Queen Anne dies at age thirty-seven; Louis marries Mary Tudor, the eighteen-year-old sister of Henry VIII, then abdicates in favor of his cousin, Francis I
1515	Francis I declares himself king of Milan; he invites Leonardo da Vinci to Amboise and gives him a house at Clos-Lucé
1516	Boumois castle built by René de Thory
1516–21	Construction of the Francis I wing at Blois, also the Façade of the Loges
1518–29	Gilles Berthelot commissions Azay-le-Rideau from an unknown architect
1519	Death of Leonardo at Clos-Lucé; Francis I begins work on Chambord
1524	On death of first wife, Francis marries Eleanor, sister of Emperor Charles V; Francis takes over Chenonceaux when Bohier succumbs; Ronsard born in the manor of Possonnière
1525	Francis, defeated at Paira, is taken as prisoner to Spain; returns one year later
1532	Villandry, with its terraced gardens, reconstructed by Le Breton, architect of Chambord
1535	Pierre Trinqueau builds Villegongis for Jacques de Beaumont-Brisay and Avoye de Chabannes
1539	Francis receives his enemy, Charles V, at Amboise castle
1540	Jacques d'Estampes has Valençay built
1547	Francis dies; Henry II, husband of Catherine de Médicis, assumes throne; he gives Chenonceaux to his mistress Diane de Poitiers
1548	Henry's son Francis betrothed to Mary Stuart
1552	Treaty giving Metz, Toul, and Verdun to France is ratified at Chambord
1559	Death of Henry II; Catherine reclaims Chenonceaux and gives Diane de Poitiers Chaumont
1560	Amboise Conspiracy and Huguenot uprising; death of Francis II
1562	Prince of Condé occupies Orleans; Catherine meets him at Tours; Duke of Guise assassinated
1572	St. Batholomew's Day Massacre of Huguenots
1574	Charles IX succeeded by his brother, Henry III; *fêtes champêtres* held at Chenonceaux
1576	Estates-General meets at Blois
1588	Second meeting of the Estates-General at Blois; duke of Guise assassinated
1589	Catherine de Médicis dies; Henry III murdered
1598	Henry IV signs Edict of Nantes
1602	Maximilien de Béthune buys castle of Sully
1617	Marie de Médicis consigned to Blois by her son, Louis XIII; she later makes her escape
1619	High constable of Luynes buys Maillé castle
1621	Armand du Plessis buys Richelieu's castle
1634	Château of Cheverny completed
1635–38	Gaston d'Orléans begins work on the wing of Blois that bears his name; work halts when Louis XIII's wife finally gives birth to a son and Gaston no longer stands in succession to throne
1682	Louis XIV moves court from Loire to Versailles
1710	Voltaire stays at Sully, presents plays there
1762	Jesuits expelled from La Flèche, which becomes a military academy
1768	Creation of the riding school at Saumur
1778	Construction of pagoda at Chanteloup
1788	Blois, condemned to demolition by revolutionary council, spared because it is needed as barracks; Chenonceaux spared altogether—because it serves as "a bridge"
1803	Talleyrand buys château of Valençay
1857	Château of Angers acquired for the nation
1873	Henry V moves to Chambord
1905	State assumes responsibility for Azay-le-Rideau
1906	Villandry bought by Dr. Carvalho, who begins the restoration of its sixteenth-century gardens
1911	French government buys Montsoreau
1930	Chambord acquired by the government
1938	Chaumont becomes state property
1952	First *son et lumière* show held at Chambord
1963	Fontevrault, long a prison, restored

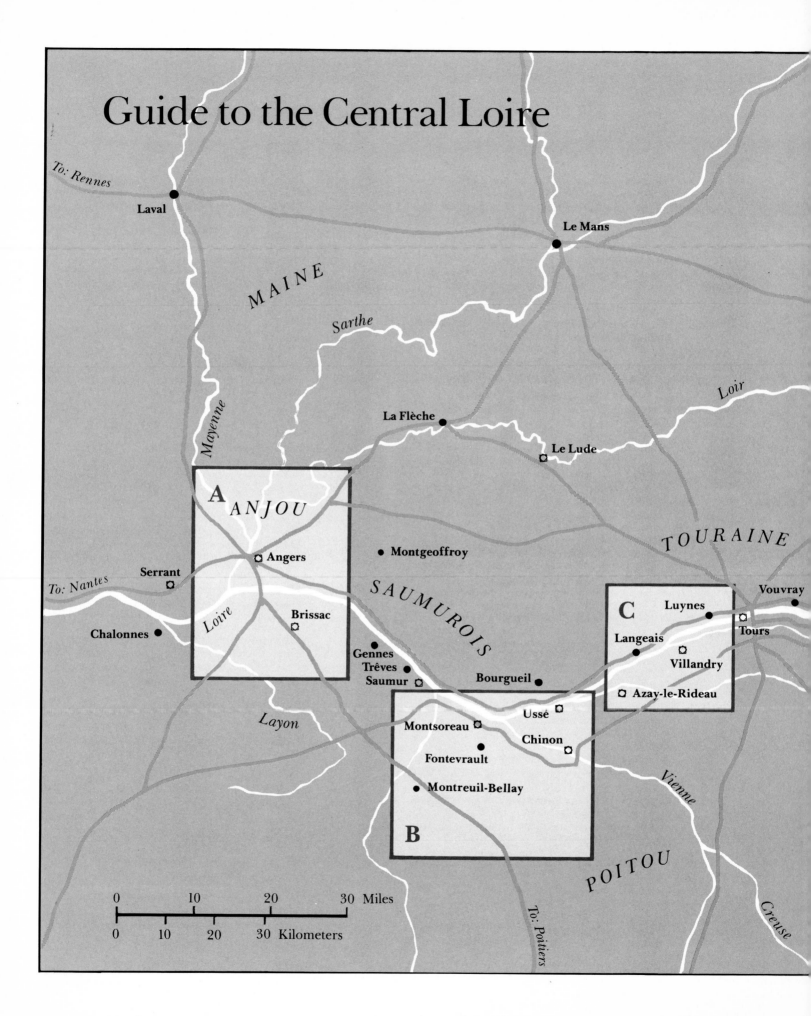

Guide to the Central Loire

To: Rennes

Laval

Le Mans

MAINE

Sarthe

Loir

La Flèche

Le Lude

A *ANJOU*

To: Nantes

Serrant

Angers

Montgeoffroy

TOURAINE

SAUMUROIS

Vouvray

C

Luynes

Loire

Brissac

Langeais

Tours

Chalonnes

Villandry

Gennes

Trêves

Saumur

Bourgueil

Azay-le-Rideau

Layon

Ussé

Montsoreau

Chinon

Fontevrault

Vienne

Montreuil-Bellay

B

POITOU

To: Poitiers

Creuse

0	10	20	30 Miles

0	10	20	30 Kilometers

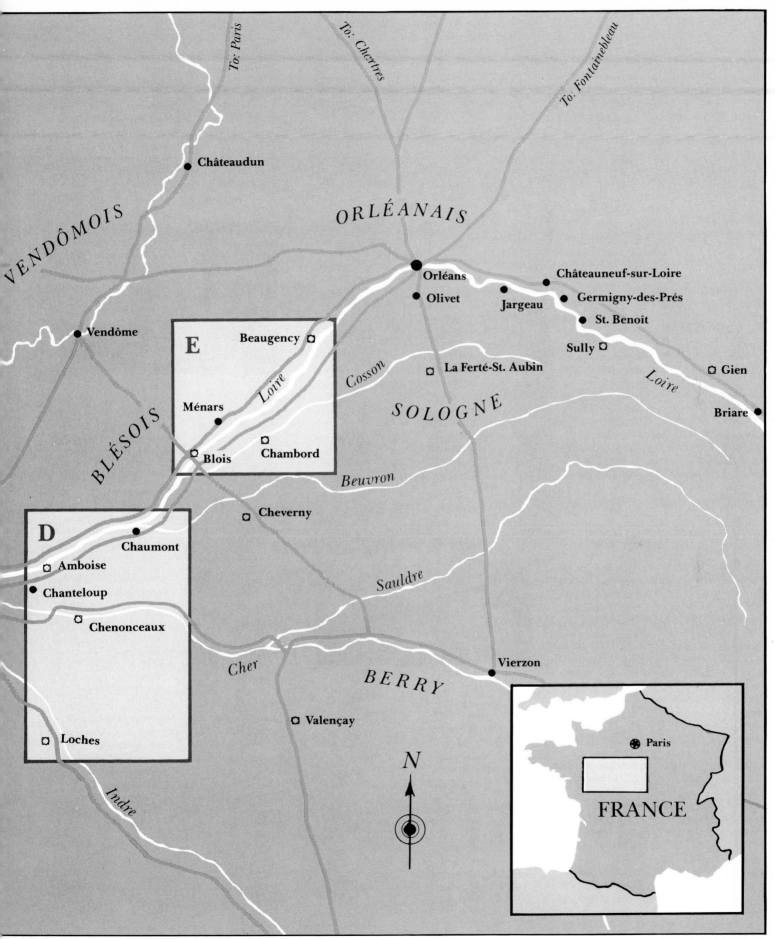

VENDÔMOIS

Châteaudun

ORLÉANAIS

To: Paris

To: Chartres

To: Fontainebleau

Orléans

Châteauneuf-sur-Loire

Olivet

Jargeau

Germigny-des-Prés

St. Benoît

Sully

Vendôme

E

Beaugency

Loire

Cosson

La Ferté-St. Aubin

Gien

BLÉSOIS

Ménars

SOLOGNE

Briare

Blois

Chambord

Loire

Beuvron

Cheverny

D

Chaumont

Amboise

Sauldre

Chanteloup

Chenonceaux

Cher

Vierzon

BERRY

Loches

Valençay

Indre

N

Paris

FRANCE

Wilhelmina Reyinga

Even the most abbreviated guides to the Loire contain scores of entries—and the most comprehensive contain hundreds. In addition to the grand châteaux themselves, the region boasts great abbeys and modest manor houses, crumbling donjons and Classical villas, Roman ruins dating from the first century B.C. and elegant country retreats dating from the first decades of this century. In short, the central Loire valley is an archaeological and architectural trove of unparalleled richness, and no short guide to the region can do more than suggest the extent of that wealth.

It would be futile, in this limited space, to attempt even a truncated catalog of the Loire's treasures. Confined to the third letter of the alphabet alone, a cataloger could easily fill these columns with highlights from the histories of Chambord, Chanteloup, Chaumont, Chenonceaux, Cheverny, and Chinon—and at that he would be omitting Cinq-Mars-le-Pile, Cunault, Champigny-sur-Veude, Cléry, and Châteauneuf. In lieu of a true Baedeker to the central Loire valley, then, we offer five separate "excursions," keyed to the map on pages 164–65 and labeled **A** through **E**. Taken together, they will provide the armchair traveler with a fuller understanding of the magnitude and the multifariousness of the Loire's legacy. Taken separately, they will provide the seasoned traveler with five potential day-trips—and suggest a dozen more.

SECTION A

Angers, at the heart of Section **A**, was for seventeen centuries the capital of Anjou and the political epicenter of the Loire valley. As such, it saw more than its share of battle and bloodshed: battlements raised by Angers' occupants were razed by those seeking to occupy the ancient settlement, only to be raised anew—as the varying courses of the château's fortifications attest. The city's Celtic founders, the Andegavi, abandoned it to the Romans in the first century B.C.; refusing to submit to Julius Caesar's *pax romana*, they carried their rebellion into the surrounding woods, where they held out for years against the better-armed invaders.

Over the next nine centuries Angers came under repeated attack by the Normans, who used their shallow-draft *drakkars* to raid with impunity along the Loire. In 867 these descendants of the Vikings at last succeeded in capturing the great keep, and they held the city for six years before being driven out by Charles the Bald, who had recently inherited Angers and the entire Loire valley from his grandfather, Charlemagne.

Thereafter Angers was ruled by the region's first great dynasty, the counts of Anjou, whose number included a tyrant often compared with Ivan the Terrible, Fulk the Black. In every respect a creature of excess, Fulk led repeated sorties against his neighbors at Tours and Blois—and, in the process, earned a reputation for cruelty and bloodlust. The Black Count's warmongering alternated with bouts of exaggerated remorse and piety, during which Fulk did public penance and endowed numerous ecclesiastical buildings, among them two monasteries in Angers.

One of Fulk's descendants, Geoffrey, married Matilda, granddaughter of William the Conqueror—and their son, through his marriage to Eleanor of Aquitaine, became master of the Loire as well as king of England. Henry II made Angers the seat of the Plantagenets, and so did his less colorful but more durable Capetian successors. The last Angevin dynasty, that of the dukes of Anjou, is remembered less for its military conquests in Italy than for its patronage of the arts—which achieved its apotheosis under Good King René, last of his line. René, a polymath and poet, musician and composer, ruled Angers for much of the mid-fifteenth century, and during that period he worked tirelessly to beautify his capital. It was he who bequeathed the famed *Apocalypse Tapestry*,

Angers

the château's greatest treasure, to his beloved city.

The massive, semicylindrical towers of Angers' famed château owe their existence to a happy accident. During the sixteenth-century Wars of Religion, King Henry III ordered the fortress destroyed, and the top two stories of the 200-foot-high towers were removed before the king's sudden death brought a halt to the demolition. The surviving battlements, slate on a foundation of white stone, are prime examples of feudal architecture. Within the château itself is a museum containing the finest display of Flemish tapestries to be

found in the Loire valley. Equally noteworthy is the nearby Cathedral of St. Maurice, its nave roofed with the first Gothic vaulting erected in Anjou, its north aisle lit by superb twelfth-century stained-glass windows.

Due south of Angers, on the road to Poitiers, is the château of **Brissac**, which was one of the region's major strongholds in the Middle Ages. Little remains of the original, eleventh-century structure, but two thick-walled guard towers connected by a sentry walk have been incorporated into the fabric of the châ-

Brissac

teau. The central pavilion, built at the beginning of the sixteenth century, rises three stories above a terrace, with the middle section lifting two additional stories to a huge lantern in the style of Louis XIII. Since 1502, when Brissac was acquired by Charles de Cossé, a governor of Paris who was later to become Marshal of France, the château has remained in the hands of his descendants: and this continuity of ownership accounts for the structure's remarkable state of preservation and fine furnishings.

SECTION B

Montsoreau, just downstream from the confluence of the Loire and the Vienne, roughly halfway from Angers to Tours, was built in the 1440s by Jean de Chambes, a major-domo to Joan of Arc's dauphin, Charles VII. A full array of machicolations and battlements give the château a forbidding appearance from the outside, but the interiors are quite comfortable, even graceful. The present structure has important historical associations—a descendant of Chambes masterminded the slaughter of the Huguenots at Angers and Saumur in the wake of the St. Bartholomew's Day Massacre—but its most remarkable association is literary: Alexander Dumas based his novel *The Lady of Montsoreau*, a section of which appears in "The Loire in Literature," upon an incident that occured at the château in the late sixteenth century. The master of Montsoreau, it seems, was blessed with a beautiful wife, Françoise, whose comeliness caught the roving eye of the governor of Anjou. Françoise spurned his advances—and the governor retaliated by spreading the word that he had seduced her. Enraged, her husband encouraged her to agree to an assignation with her reputed lover on the banks of the Loire opposite the château—where the braggart was promptly dispatched by the man he claimed to have cuckolded. Montsoreau, abandoned at the time of the Revolution and broken up after that, has been admirably restored over the past half century; its attractions include a museum devoted to souvenirs of France's conquest of Morocco.

It is reliably reported that Charles Perrault, seventeenth-century author of the *Mother Goose Tales*, had the huge château of **Ussé**, east of Montsoreau, in mind when he wrote "The Sleeping Beauty"—and as one approaches this crenelated and turreted structure from the Loire embankment, it is not hard to see why. Ussé is somewhat daunting,

Ussé

both in its bulk and its battlements, but this formidable fortress stands on a many-leveled terrace that is banked with flowers. These soften the austerity of the château itself, and the overall effect is more enchanting than forbidding—precisely what we expect a fairytale castle to be. Ussé, which was begun in the fifteenth century and completed in the eighteenth, is an amalgam of architectural styles: the east block is Gothic; the west, Renaissance; the south, transitional from Gothic to Classical. Of particular interest is the chapel, which stands by itself in the park surrounding the château; erected between 1520 and 1538 by Charles d'Espinay for his wife, Lucrèce de Pons, it is a Renaissance gem emblazoned with a repeating motif, the initials C and L intertwined.

Ussé is remarkably well-preserved and extensively restored; **Chinon**, a few miles to the southwest, is little more than a blasted shell—yet no one interested in the history of the Loire valley can afford to pass by this sprawling fortress overlooking the Vienne. No castle in the entire valley is as rich in history or as steeped in tragedy as Chinon, which is actually three châteaux in one.

Chinon

The most southerly of these, now partially dismantled, is known as Fort St. Georges and was erected at the behest of Henry II, who died there in 1189. (Legend has it that his son and successor, Richard the Lion-Hearted, also died at Chinon, brought there from a battlefield near Limoges where he had taken an arrow in the shoulder. The wound was slight, but the valiant warrior-king developed blood poisoning and died on April 6, 1199.)

A moat connects Fort St. Georges, named by its builder for the patron saint of England, to the Château du Milieu, where the hapless dauphin, Charles VII, made his court in the early decades of the fifteenth century. It was here that Joan of Arc sought out the dauphin, who received the eighteen-year-old peasant girl in the great hall of the château, which was lit for the occasion by dozens of torches.

During the month she remained at Chinon before departing for Orléans, Joan lived in the third major structure on the escarpment, the Château du Coudray, which is dominated by a donjon erected by King Phillip of France in 1205. Following Joan's victories at Orléans and elsewhere, the French court was able to abandon Chinon, which eventually passed into the hands of Cardinal Richelieu. It belonged to his family until the Revolution, but they took little interest in the ancient structure, which deteriorated badly. Not until the Napoleonic era were its crumbling fortifications repaired and consolidated, and by then little was left but the keep and the curtain wall.

Shortly after Henry II's death at Chinon his remains were transferred to the abbey of **Fontevrault**, a few miles to the west. Interred there at his specific instructions, he became the first English king ever buried on foreign soil, a distinction extended to his son Richard a decade later. The transept of Fontevrault, an austerely elegant Romanesque structure consecrated by Pope Calixtus II in 1119, also contains the polychrome sarcophagus of Henry's wife, Eleanor of Aquitaine, and the effigy erected in memory of one of their daughters-in-law, Isabelle of Angoulême. These alone would make the abbey church and its adjoining cloister worth a visit, but they are not the sole attractions of Fontevrault. The kitchen tower, an octagonal structure nearly ninety feet high, is a marvel of medieval masonry: its five wood-burning fireplaces and twenty chimneys are thoroughly functional yet altogether elegant, an exquisite solution to a mundane problem.

Interestingly enough, there is an echo of Fontevrault's kitchen tower a few miles to the west, where the château of **Montreuil-Bellay** incorporates a kitchen wing that is likewise octagonal and rises to a central chimney. Smaller in scale and less heavily ornamented, the kitchen tower of Montreuil-Bellay may be thought of as the country cousin of its more famous relative at Fontevrault. Another interesting feature of the so-called Petit Château at Montreuil-Bellay is its residential wing, which is actually four entirely separate dwellings, each with its own entryway and turreted stairs. The Château Neuf, a fifteenth-century addition to the castle complex, contains many splendidly decorated rooms and a frescoed oratory.

Saumur, which stands on the Loire just above the northern edge of Section

Saumur

B, is well worth the slight detour an excursion to this medieval stronghold involves. The château itself has been extensively restored and looks remarkably like the miniature of Saumur castle that appears in the duke de Berri's incomparable *Très Riches Heures*. The rival dynasties of Blois and Anjou vied for possession of the castle for generations, but Saumur won its lasting reputation as a great center of Protestantism in the sixteenth and seventeenth centuries. Under the aegis of Governor Duplessis-Mornay, known as "the Pope of the Huguenots," the castle's fortifications were extended and strengthened, and during the reign of the Sun King, Louis XIV, those strong walls served as a royal prison. Today those same walls enclose two remarkable museums: the Musée d'Arts Décoratifs, which contains an especially fine collection of seventeenth-century enamels and porcelain as well as fabrics and furniture of the period; and the Musée du Cheval, or Equine Museum.

SECTION C

Section **C** lies just west of **Tours**, the geographical heart of the central Loire valley. This most attractive and intriguing of Loire-side cities is itself worth at least a full day of any traveler's time, for Tours was the birthplace of French Christianity under St. Martin and a vaunted center of Christian learning under Charlemagne. Moreover, Tours is a convenient staging-base for sight-seeing expeditions to the west of the city.

Six miles downstream from Tours—and on the opposite bank of the Loire—is the thirteenth-century *château-fort* of **Luynes**, once the proud possession of Charles d'Albert, Duke of Luynes and counsellor to King Louis XIII. Although partially dismantled, the curtain wall of this feudal keep is nonetheless prepossessing; the château itself has fallen into disrepair, however, and is not open to the public.

In a sense Luynes is a minor-key prelude to **Langeais**, which lies further west along the same bank of the Loire and which is, in all respects, a more magnificent sight. Situated at a strategic point along the Angers-Tours highway, Langeais was to play an important role in the military history of the region—first as a Roman *castrum*; then as a link in the chain of fortifications constructed by Fulk the Black; and later as an English command post during the Hundred Years' War. The English left Langeais in a sorry state, and when Jean Bourré, the treasurer of France under Louis XI, took over the ruined castle in 1465, he tore down what remained and built a new château on the site. That task took a mere four years—virtually overnight, by contemporary standards. As a result, Langeais possesses a unity of style that is unique among Loire valley châteaux: it incorporates no earlier structures and it has suffered no significant accretions. The castle's great hall, remarkable for its Gothic furnishings and Flemish tapestries, was the scene of Charles VIII and Anne of Brittany's marriage in 1491.

Azay-le-Rideau, south of Langeais, is permanently—and tragically—associated with Charles VIII's predecessor and namesake, the hapless dauphin Charles VII. As suspicious as he was insecure, Charles thought he heard a member of the Burgundian guard at Azay insult him as he rode through the hamlet in 1418—and he immediately ordered the execution of all 350 members of the castle's garrison and the torching of the fort itself. For the next century the blackened ruins were known as Azay-le-Brûlé—"Azay the Burnt." Then in 1518 the financier Gilles Berthelot built a new château on the site. Gothic in form but Renaissance in its appointments, Azay-le-Rideau is one of the supreme achievements of sixteenth-century French architecture: harmonious in its overall design, it is also harmoniously situated on the banks of the river Indre.

Villandry, north and east of Azay-le-Rideau, also dates from the early six-

Villandry

teenth century, but there the similarity between the two châteaux ends. One visits Azay for its architectural perfection; Villandry, for its gardens—a perfect recreation of the sort of formal gardens that surrounded all Loire valley châteaux when these two were built. The magnificent plantings at Villandry owe their existence to the château's nineteenth century owners, the Carvallo family, who created and maintained the building's three-level garden. As was commonly the case with sixteenth-century gardens, these are divided into a kitchen garden, and ornamental garden of topiary and box borders, and a *jardin d'eau*, or water garden, that covers some 8,400 square yards. In the lowest of these, the kitchen garden, vegetables are planted in square beds bordered by carefully trimmed box and yew hedges. One tier up is the pleasure garden with its flower beds and formal borders laid out in the strictest geometric patterns. The water garden, which is topmost, includes reflecting pools, cascades, fountains, and pergolas.

SECTION D

Not altogether by coincidence, Section **D**, halfway between Tours and Blois, includes several of the most interesting châteaux in the Loire valley. This is a heavily forested area, which made it attactive to noble huntsmen over the centuries; it is also a strategically important stretch of the valley, which made it important to noble conquerors. **Loches**, for instance, was a fortified keep from earliest times: it was erected by the counts of Anjou in the eleventh century, and it was continuously reinforced thereafter, both by the Plantagenets and the Capetians. No modern visitor can fail to be impressed by the results, which include a double perimeter wall inset with massive, semicylindrical towers; ramparts nearly a mile in length; and a 121-foot-high keep that was long considered the strongest in the entire valley. Ironically, this most imposing of donjons is associated with two lovely women—Agnès Sorel, mistress of Charles VII, who was buried within the castle walls; and Anne of Brittany, Charles VIII's queen, who found Loches a perfect retreat from the demands of court life.

Of **Chanteloup**, built by the duke of Choiseul in imitation of Versailles, nothing remains except a 144-foot-high stone pagoda that once graced the château's gardens. **Amboise**, a few miles distant, has likewise suffered depredations since the Revolution, but this château was larger to begin with, and more remains. What the tourist to Amboise finds on the roughly triangular castle mount is a block of royal apartments known as the Logis du Roi and a small oratory, once part of the queen's apartments, called the Chapel of St. Hubert. Both are superb examples of the Flamboyant Gothic style. What the visitor will not find is the château of Charles VIII's day, a warren of private apartments and public reception rooms that entirely enclosed the castle terrace. It is said that Charles had hundreds of tapestries hung from the walls of the buildings surrounding this courtyard on festival days, and that a vast, sky-blue awning was suspended above the courtyard to protect revelers from the elements. This luxury-loving monarch furnished Amboise with acquisitions from his numerous trips abroad, where he also recruited architects, sculptors, tailors and gardeners. The result was an era of unparalleled opulence in Loire

Amboise

valley history, an era that came to an abrupt end in 1498, when Charles died as the result of a blow to the head suffered in a freakish domestic accident.

The histories of Chaumont and Chenonceaux are linked by one name, that of Catherine de Médicis, wife of Henry II of France. **Chaumont**, which was built and rebuilt several times in the fifteenth and early sixteenth centuries by members of Amboise family, was acquired in 1560 by Catherine, who made the château an instrument of revenge against her late husband's mistress, Diane de Poitiers. Chaumont, which stands on a high rise above the Loire, is a not unlovely structure, although its aspect is distinctly feudal and unadorned. It is distinctly less handsome than **Chenonceaux**, however—which is often said to be the lovliest of all Loire châteaux. Catherine de Médicis felt this, certainly; and so she felt especially stung when her husband awarded Chenonceaux to Diane de Poitiers in 1547. During his

Chenonceaux

lifetime there was little Catherine could do about this, but when Henry died in 1559 his widow wasted little time in reasserting her rights: she acquired Chaumont with one purpose in mind—to force her longtime rival to accept it as a "gift" and relinquish Chenonceaux to her. It was Catherine who added the two-story gallery to the châteaux—the "bridge" across the Cher that is Chenonceaux's most distinctive feature. It was here that Catherine's son Henry III held the extravagant balls and elaborate masquerades that were the chief feature of his dissolute reign; and it was here, after Catherine's death, that Henry's widow, Louise of Lorraine, spent her last days in a black-draped room, mourning the death of a husband who had never loved her.

The immense château of **Blois**, in the southwest corner of Section **E**, is by no means the handsomest of Loire valley châteaux, but it is in many ways the most fascinating. From the fourteenth through the seventeenth centuries, the history of Blois is inextricable from the history of France, and this hulking *château-fort* is as ghost-ridden and blood-drenched as any in the valley. During the sixteenth-century reigns of Louis XII and Francis I, Blois was the seat of the French court—rightly known, in retrospect, as the Versailles of the Renaissance. Francis would eventually relocate the court to the east, in a grandiose new château built to his specifications, but the States-General would continue to meet at Blois, and there the meddlesome duke de Guise would meet his death in 1588, falling under the blades of hired assassins. Visitors to the so-called Francis I Wing at Blois can trace the ill-fated duke's movements on that unhappy day—from the Council Chamber to the King's Bedroom to the Old Study and back again. These second-floor chambers are reached by the Grand Staircase that is the wing's outstanding architectural feature. An open-work octagon that served as a lookout and multilevel balcony, this staircase is attributed to Jacques Sourdeau, who also worked on Chambord, the grandest of all Loire valley châteaux.

Chambord is an awesome creation, but then Francis I was an awe-inspiring king. A man of seemingly limitless appetites who did nothing by half measures, Francis commanded his architects to build him a new castle, one befitting the mightiest of Renaissance princes. What his architects gave him was Chambord: 400 rooms, 100 staircases, 800 capitals, 365 chimneys, and a 105-foot-high lan-

tern surmounting it all. Set in a private preserve of more than 13,600 acres—11,000 of them woodland—Chambord was a huntsman's delight; and Francis, who interrupted his own honeymoon to participate in a day-long hunt, was clearly delighted by his new castle. His successors did not share his enthusiasm—for hunting or for Chambord, so far from the great cultural centers of the Loire valley—and after Francis' death the mighty château fell into disrepair. As a result, it is almost bare of furniture today, stripped back to the bones created by the royal architects of the 1500s.

The same is true of the small château of **Beaugency**, which has a keep as old as that of Loches and associations with Eleanor of Aquitaine (whose first marriage, to Louis VII of France, was annulled there) and Joan of Arc (who relieved the city in 1429). But this château now contains an excellent regional museum, one especially strong in native Orléanais costumes and furniture.

Ménars, southwest of Beaugency along the same bank of the Loire, is also associated with a noblewoman—in this case the marquise de Pompadour, who acquired the seventeenth-century château in 1760. It was only one of a dozen châteaux given to Mme de Pompadour by her erstwhile lover and longtime confidant, Louis XIV, but it had the distinction of being the last. Ménars was a modest country seat when it came into the marquise's hands, but she soon set about transforming it. However, the special attraction of this château is not

Ménars

the building itself but its gardens: lawns lined with box trees, orange groves, and an ivy-covered Lovers' Temple with a rounded cupola.

Blois, Chambord, Beaugency, Ménars. Taken together, they are an ambitious day-tour; taken separately, each could profitably occupy a full day of any visitor's time. Yet they are only a sampling of the riches to be found in Section E, just as sections **A** through **E** are but a sampling of the treasures to be found in the central Loire.

Selected Bibliography

Broderick, Alan H., ed. *Touraine, with Anjou and Maine.* London: Hodder and Stoughton, 1948

Bullogh, Donald. *The Age of Charlemagne.* New York: G.P. Putnam's Sons, 1966.

Cook, Theodore A. *Old Touraine: The Life and History of the Château of the Loire.* 2 vols. London: Rivingtons, 1903.

Dunlop, Ian. *Château of the Loire.* New York: Taplinger, 1969.

Goldring, Douglas. *The Loire: The Record of a Pilgrimage from Gerbier de Joncs to St. Nazaire.* London: Constable and Co., Ltd., 1913.

Harvey, John H. *The Plantagenets.* London: B.T. Batsford, 1948.

Hibbert, Christopher. *The Grand Tour.* New York: G.P. Putnam's Sons, 1969.

James, Henry. *A Little Tour in France.* Cambridge: John Wilson and Son, 1884.

Kelly, Amy. *Eleanor of Aquitaine and the Four Kings.* Cambridge: Harvard University Press, 1950.

MacColl, Averill. *The Loire.* London: Oxford University Press, 1965.

Martin-Demézil, Jean. *The Loire Valley and Its Treasures.* London: Allen and Unwin, 1969.

Michelin Guide to the Châteaux of the Loire. London: The Dickens Press. 1964.

Pépin, Eugène. *The Glory of the Loire.* (Trans. by Thomas Wikeley.) New York: The Viking Press, 1971.

Poisson, Georges. *Châteaux de la Loire.* Paris: Larousse, 1963.

Rowe, Vivian. *The Loire.* Washington: Robert B. Luce, Inc., 1969.

Acknowledgements and Picture Credits

The title or description of each picture appears after the page number (boldface), followed by its location. Photographic credits appear in parentheses. The following abbreviations are used:

BN,P—Bibliothèque Nationale, Paris
(SK)—Sylvain Knecht
(AW)—Adam Woolfitt-Woodfin Camp, Inc.

ENDPAPERS Tapestry, *La Vie Seigneuriale*, Loire Valley. BN,P HALF TITLE Symbol designed by Jay J. Smith Studio FRONTISPIECE Chambord. (AW) **9** *Agnes Sorel*, Loches. (SK) **10–11** Chambord. (AW) **12** Saumur **13** Poitiers. Both: *Tres Riches Heures* . . . , Ms. 65 fols. 9v & 7v. Musée Condé, Chantilly.

CHAPTER 1 **15** Langeais. (SK) **16** (Rosine Mazin, TOP) **17** G.C. Wachten, Voltaire medallion. Voltaire Institute, Geneva **18** Quentin de La Tour, *Mme de Pompadour*. Louvre **19** (AW) **20** (SK) **21** top (AW) bottom (Roger-Viollet) **22–23** (AW) **25** (AW) **26** (SK) **28** Apocalypse Tapestry, detail *Adoration du Lepreux*, 1376. Musée des Tapisseries, Angers. (Luc Joubert/American Heritage) **29** Overall: (SK) bottom (SK)

CHAPTER 2 **31** Bronze horseman. Louvre **32–33** (AW) **34** Baptism of Clovis, *Vie de St. Denys*, 13th century. BN,P **35** (Archives Photographiques) **36** (SK) **38** *Alcuin and Charlemagne*. Ms. Inv. 3927 fol 1 Kestner Museum, Hannover **39** *La Chronique de Brabant*, 16th century. BN,P **41** *Bible of Charles the Bald*, ca. 846. BN,P Ms. Latin 1, fol 423.

CHAPTER 3 **43** Blois. (Roger-Viollet) **44** (AW) **45** (SK) **46** *Henry II*. BN,P **47** Mirror case, 14th century. Victoria and Albert Museum **48–49** (SK) **49** *Peterborough Psalter*. Bibliothèque Royale, Brussels Ms. 9961, fol 33a. **50** *King John Hunting* **51** *Henry II with Thomas à Becket*. Both: British Museum. Ms. Cotton Claudius D. II fols 113 and 70. **52–53** (Bruno Barbey, Magnum) **56–57** Both: (SK) **59** (AW)

CHAPTER 4 **61** Blois. (Roger-Viollet) **62** Tomb of King Edward IV, Canterbury Cathedral. **63** Froissart, *Battle of Poitiers, Chroniques*. Musée Condé, Chantilly Ms. 873. (Giraudon) **64** *Charles V*, 14th century. Louvre (American Heritage) **66** *Battle of Agincourt, Chroniques de France*. BN,P Ms. 2680. fol 208. **67** Henry V **68–69** Register of the Council of the Parliament of Paris, 1429. Archives Nationales, Paris (Giraudon) **70–71** (AW) **73** Orléans, 15th century. BN,P **74** Fouquet, *Charles VII*. Louvre **75** View of Orléans

CHAPTER 5 **77** Blois. (Roger-Viollet) **78–79** (AW) **80** *Louis XII*. **81** *Anne of Brittany*, ca. 1500. Both: Metropolitan Museum of Art, Blumenthal Bequest, 1941 **82** Clouet, *François I*, Louvre (Giraudon) **83** (SK) **84** Leonardo da Vinci, *Self-portrait*. By Gracious Permission of Her Majesty Queen Elizabeth II **85** (Pierre Jahan/American Heritage) **86** bottom BN,P **86** top and **87** (AW) **88–89** Engraving after Van der Meulen. BN,P **89** Engraving by Aveline. BN,P **91** (Rosine Mazin, TOP) **92** Floorplan. British Museum Engravings. BN,P **93** (SK) **95** (SK)

CHAPTER 6 **97** Blois. (SK) **98** (Bruno Barbey, Magnum) **99** Clouet, *Diane de Poitiers*. National Gallery of Art, Kress Collection **100** Both: (AW) **101** Perrissin, *Execution at Amboise*, 1560. Bildarchiv Nationalbibliothek, Vienna **102–103** (Bruno Barbey, Magnum) **103** *Francis II and Mary Stuart*, 1558. Metropolitan Museum of Art **105** (Bruno Barbey, Magnum) **106–107** F. Clouet, *Henry III, Elizabeth of Austria, Charles IX*. All: BN,P (Giraudon) **108–109** *Massacre of St. Bartholomew*. Kunsthistorisches Museum, Vienna **110** left Jean Rabal, *Louise de Lorraine*, 1575. BN,P right BN,P **112–13** (Bruno Barbey, Magnum)

CHAPTER 7 **115** Cleveland Museum of Art **117** Gaston d'Orleans, *Variae . . . Species Diverses Fleurs . . .*, Paris, 1660. Hunt Botanical Garden. **119** (Bulloz) **120** (SK) **121** (AW) **122–23** Both: (SK) **126–27** Both: (SK)

CHAPTER 8 **129** Amboise. (Roger-Viollet) **130–31** (AW) **132–33** Both: (Photo Arsicaud, Tours) **134** (AW) **135** top Both: (AW) bottom: (SK)

LOIRE IN LITERATURE: **136** Chambord. (Roger-Viollet) **138–39** Blois. (Roger-Viollet) **139** Diagram of Blois. (Archives Photographiques) **140–41** Chamont. (Roger-Viollet) **145** Charleval. BN,P **149** Amboise. (SK) **150** top Diagram of Amboise. (Archives Photographiques) bottom (SK) **155** Fontevrault. (SK) **156–57** Chenonceaux. (Roger-Viollet) **158–59** top Diagram of Chenonceaux. BN,P bottom Chenonceaux. (Roger-Viollet) REFERENCE **164–65** Map of the Loire Valley by Wilhelmina Reyinga **166–69** All: Sylvain Knecht

Index